PROPERTY OF STRATUS
WESTERN DEVELOPMENT CENTER

UNIX® SYSTEM V RELEASE 4

Device Driver Interface/ Driver-Kernel Interface (DDI/DKI) Reference Manual

UNIX Software Operation

Copyright 1990, 1989, 1988, 1987, 1986, 1985, 1984, 1983 AT&T
All Rights Reserved
Printed in USA

Published by Prentice-Hall, Inc.
A Division of Simon & Schuster
Englewood Cliffs, New Jersey 07632

No part of this publication may be reproduced or transmitted in any form or by any means—graphic, electronic, electrical, mechanical, or chemical, including photocopying, recording in any medium, taping, by any computer or information storage and retrieval systems, etc., without prior permissions in writing from AT&T.

IMPORTANT NOTE TO USERS

While every effort has been made to ensure the accuracy of all information in this document, AT&T assumes no liability to any party for any loss or damage caused by errors or omissions or by statements of any kind in this document, its updates, supplements, or special editions, whether such errors are omissions or statements resulting from negligence, accident, or any other cause. AT&T further assumes no liability arising out of the application or use of any product or system described herein; nor any liability for incidental or consequential damages arising from the use of this document. AT&T disclaims all warranties regarding the information contained herein, whether expressed, implied or statutory, *including implied warranties of merchantability or fitness for a particular purpose.* AT&T makes no representation that the interconnection of products in the manner described herein will not infringe on existing or future patent rights, nor do the descriptions contained herein imply the granting or license to make, use or sell equipment constructed in accordance with this description.

AT&T reserves the right to make changes without further notice to any products herein to improve reliability, function, or design.

TRADEMARKS

UNIX and WE are registered trademarks of AT&T.

10 9 8 7 6 5 4 3 2 1

ISBN 0-13-933680-X

UNIX
PRESS
A Prentice Hall Title

P R E N T I C E   H A L L

ORDERING INFORMATION

UNIX® SYSTEM V, RELEASE 4 DOCUMENTATION

To order single copies of UNIX® SYSTEM V, Release 4 documentation, please call (201) 767-5937.

ATTENTION DOCUMENTATION MANAGERS AND TRAINING DIRECTORS:
For bulk purchases in excess of 30 copies please write to:
Corporate Sales
Prentice Hall
Englewood Cliffs, N.J. 07632.
Or call: (201) 592-2498.

ATTENTION GOVERNMENT CUSTOMERS: For GSA and other pricing information please call (201) 767-5994.

Prentice-Hall International (UK) Limited, *London*
Prentice-Hall of Australia Pty. Limited, *Sydney*
Prentice-Hall Canada Inc., *Toronto*
Prentice-Hall Hispanoamericana, S.A., *Mexico*
Prentice-Hall of India Private Limited, *New Delhi*
Prentice-Hall of Japan, Inc., *Tokyo*
Simon & Schuster Asia Pte. Ltd., *Singapore*
Editora Prentice-Hall do Brasil, Ltda., *Rio de Janeiro*

AT&T UNIX® System V Release 4

General Use and System Administration

UNIX® System V Release 4 Network User's and Administrator's Guide
UNIX® System V Release 4 Product Overview and Master Index
UNIX® System V Release 4 System Administrator's Guide
UNIX® System V Release 4 System Administrator's Reference Manual
UNIX® System V Release 4 User's Guide
UNIX® System V Release 4 User's Reference Manual

General Programmer's Series

UNIX® System V Release 4 Programmer's Guide: ANSI C
  and Programming Support Tools
UNIX® System V Release 4 Programmer's Guide: Character User Interface
  (FMLI and ETI)
UNIX® System V Release 4 Programmer's Guide: Networking Interfaces
UNIX® System V Release 4 Programmer's Guide: POSIX Conformance
UNIX® System V Release 4 Programmer's Guide: System Services
  and Application Packaging Tools
UNIX® System V Release 4 Programmer's Reference Manual

System Programmer's Series

UNIX® System V Release 4 ANSI C Transition Guide
UNIX® System V Release 4 BSD / XENIX® Compatibility Guide
UNIX® System V Release 4 Device Driver Interface / Driver−Kernel
  Interface (DDI / DKI) Reference Manual
UNIX® System V Release 4 Migration Guide
UNIX® System V Release 4 Programmer's Guide: STREAMS

Available from Prentice Hall

Contents

1 Introduction
About This Document 1-1
Organization of Driver Reference Manuals 1-7
Conventions Used in This Document 1-8
Related Learning Materials 1-9

2 Driver Entry Points (D2)
Introduction 2-1
Overview of Driver Entry-Point Routines and Naming
    Conventions 2-2
Manual Pages 2-4

3 Kernel Functions (D3)
Introduction 3-1
Manual Pages 3-7

4 Data Structures (D4)
Introduction 4-1
Manual Pages 4-3

A Appendix A: Error Codes

Table of Contents

B   **Appendix B: Migration from Release 3.2 to Release 4.0**

Index

Permuted Index

Figures and Tables

Figure 1-1: Scope of DDI and DKI	1-1
Table 1-1: Exclusive Entry Points, Functions, and Structures	1-5
Table 1-2: Textual Conventions Used in This Book	1-8
Table 2-1: STREAMS Driver Entry Point Summary	2-2
Table 2-2: Driver Entry Points not Specific to STREAMS	2-3
Table 3-1: STREAMS Kernel Function Summary	3-2
Table 3-2: Kernel Functions Not Specific to STREAMS	3-4
Table 4-1: STREAMS Data Structure Summary	4-1
Table 4-2: Data Structures not Specific to STREAMS	4-2
Table A-1: Driver Error Codes	A-1
Table A-2: Error Codes by Driver Routine	A-2
Table B-1: 3.2 to 4.0 Migration	B-2

1. INTRODUCTION

1. INTRODUCTION

1 Introduction

About This Document	1-1
Porting	1-2
Scope of Interfaces	1-3
■ Scope of the Device Driver Interface (DDI)	1-3
■ Scope of the Driver–Kernel Interface (DKI)	1-4
Interface Members	1-5
Audience	1-5
How to Use This Document	1-6

Organization of Driver Reference Manuals	1-7

Conventions Used in This Document	1-8

Related Learning Materials	1-9
Documentation	1-9
■ Driver Development	1-9
■ STREAMS	1-10
■ C Programming Language and General Programming	1-10
■ Assembly Language	1-10
■ Operating System	1-11
■ Software Packaging	1-11
Training	1-11

About This Document

The *Device Driver Interface/Driver-Kernel Interface Reference Manual* provides reference information needed to write device drivers in the UNIX System V Release 4 environment. It describes two device driver interface specifications: the Device Driver Interface (DDI) and the Driver-Kernel Interface (DKI). Drivers written to conform to one or both of these interfaces are more likely to be portable to other environments. DDI and DKI address different aspects of the compatibility problem—their differences are summarized in Figure 1-1.

Figure 1-1: Scope of DDI and DKI

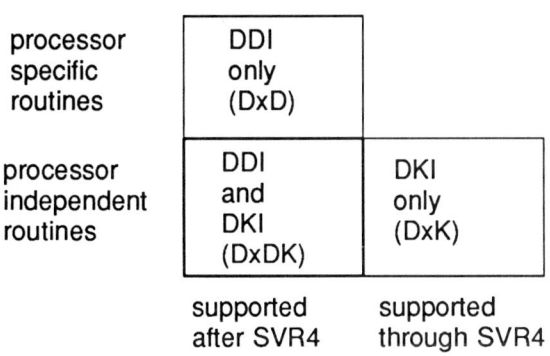

Each box in Figure 1-1 represents a different set of interfaces. The "DDI only" set (indicated throughout this manual with the D*x*D cross-reference code) are processor specific and are intended to be supported beyond Release 4.0. The DDI described in this manual is specific to the porting base, the 3B2 computer. The "DKI only" set (D*x*K cross-reference code) are processor independent, but are not guaranteed to be supported in the next release.

Most of the routines, functions, and structures described in this manual are part of both DDI and DKI (cross-referenced by D*x*DK). As Figure 1-1 shows, drivers written to conform to both interfaces are portable to all AT&T computers supporting UNIX System V Release 4, and they will be compatible through and beyond Release 4. To understand more completely what is meant by "portable" and "compatible" for DDI and DKI, the scope of each interface must be more thoroughly explained.

About This Document

The goals of DDI and DKI overlap, and are not in any way mutually exclusive. That is, a driver may be written to conform to both interfaces, increasing the chances that driver code can be ported and can remain compatible with future releases of the operating system.

Porting

Software is usually considered portable if it can be adapted to run in a different environment more cheaply than it can be rewritten. The new environment may include a different processor, operating system, and even the language in which the program is written, if a language translator is available. More often, however, software is ported between environments that share an operating system, processor, and source language. The source code is modified to accommodate the differences in compilers or processors or releases of the operating system.

In the past, device drivers did not port easily for one or more of the following reasons:

- To enhance functionality, members had been added to kernel data structures accessed by drivers, or the sizes of existing members had been redefined.

- The calling or return syntax of kernel functions had changed.

- Driver developers did not use existing kernel functions where available, or relied on undocumented side effects that were not maintained in the next release.

- Processor-specific code had been scattered throughout the driver when it could have been isolated.

Operating systems are periodically reissued to customers as a way to improve performance, fix bugs, and add new features. This is probably the most common threat to compatibility encountered by developers responsible for maintaining software. Another common problem is upgrading hardware. As new hardware is developed, customers occasionally decide to upgrade to faster, more capable computers of the same family. Although they may run the same operating system as those being replaced, processor-specific code may prevent the software from porting.

_____ About This Document

Scope of Interfaces

Although application programs have all of the porting problems mentioned, developers attempting to port device drivers have special challenges. Before describing the differences between DDI and DKI, it is necessary to understand the position of device drivers in UNIX systems.

Device drivers are kernel modules that control data transferred to and received from peripheral devices. Although drivers are configured into a UNIX system as part of the kernel, they are developed independently from the rest of the kernel. If the goal of achieving complete freedom in modifying the kernel is to be reconciled with the goal of binary compatibility with existing drivers, the interaction between drivers and the kernel must be rigorously regulated. This driver/kernel service interface is the most important of the three distinguishable interfaces for a driver, summarized as follows:

- Driver–Kernel. I/O System calls result in calls to driver entry point routines. These make up the kernel-to-driver part of the service interface, described in Section 2 of this manual. Drivers may call any of the functions described in Section 3. These are the driver-to-kernel part of the interface.

- Driver–Hardware. All drivers (except software drivers) must include an interrupt handling entry point, and may also perform direct memory access (DMA). These, and other hardware-specific interactions make up the driver/hardware interface.

- Driver–Boot/Configuration Software. At boot time, the existence of a driver is made known to the system through information in system files, enabling the system to include the driver. The interaction between the driver and the boot and configuration software is the third interface affecting drivers.

Scope of the Device Driver Interface (DDI)

The primary goal of DDI is to facilitate both source and binary portability across successive releases of UNIX System V on a particular machine. Implicit in this goal is an important fact. Although there is only one DKI, each processor product has its own DDI. Therefore, if a driver is ever to be ported to different hardware, special attention must be paid to the machine-specific routines that make up the "DDI only" part of a driver. These include but are not confined to

About This Document

the driver/hardware interface (as described in the previous section). Some processor-specific functionality also may belong to the driver/kernel interface, and may not be easy to locate.

To achieve the goal of source and binary compatibility, the functions, routines, and structures specified in a DDI must be used according to these rules.

- Drivers cannot access system state structure (for example, u and sysinfo) directly.

- For structures external to the driver that may be accessed directly, only the utility functions provided in Section 3 of this manual should be used. More generally, these functions should be used wherever possible.

- The header file ddi.h must be included at the end of the list of header files. This header file "undefines" several macros that are reimplemented as functions.

Scope of the Driver-Kernel Interface (DKI)

As its name implies, the DKI (Driver-Kernel Interface) is a defined service interface for the entry point routines and utility functions specified for communication between the driver and kernel. It does not encompass the driver/hardware or the driver/boot software interface.

Information is exchanged between the driver and kernel in the form of data structures. The DKI specifies the contents of these structures as well as the calling and return syntax of the entry points and utility functions.

The intent of DKI is to promote source portability across implementations of UNIX System V on different machines, and applies only to System V Release 4. Because DKI applies only to the driver/kernel interface, it must be understood that the sections of driver code affecting the hardware and boot/configuration interfaces may need to be rewritten, and should be isolated in subroutines as much as possible.

About This Document

 NOTE Certain interfaces documented in the DKI are not part of the DDI. Driver writers should be aware that the use of these interfaces is not guaranteed to be supported beyond System V Release 4.

Interface Members

As noted before, most entry points (Section 2), functions (Section 3), and structures (Section 4) described in this manual belong to both DDI and DKI. Table 1-1 lists the those that are exclusive either to DDI or DKI.

Table 1-1: Exclusive Entry Points, Functions, and Structures

	DDI only	DKI only
Section 2	init, int, size, start	segmap, mmap
Section 3	dma_pageio, etoimajor, getemajor, geteminor, getvec, hdeeqd, hdelog, itoemajor, kvtophys, physiock, vtop	hat_getkpfnum
Section 4	hdedata	None

Audience

This manual is for experienced C programmers responsible for creating, modifying, or maintaining drivers that run on AT&T UNIX System V Release 4 and beyond. It assumes that the reader is familiar with UNIX system internals and the advanced capabilities of the C Programming Language. See the "Related Learning Materials" section for a list of available AT&T documents and courses.

About This Document

How to Use This Document

This manual is organized into four sections and two appendixes:

- "Section 1: Introduction" introduces the DDI, DKI, and other driver interfaces, lists the notational conventions used in this document, and lists related courses and documents.

- "Section 2: Driver Entry Points" contains reference pages for all driver entry point routines.

- "Section 3: Kernel Functions" contains reference pages for all driver functions used in DDI/DKI drivers.

- "Section 4: Data Structures" contains reference pages for structures used in DDI/DKI drivers.

- "Appendix A: Error Codes" contains a list of the error codes that are appropriate for use in DDI/DKI drivers.

- "Appendix B: Migration from Release 3.2 to Release 4.0" describes the changes to DDI/DKI between Release 3.2 and Release 4.0 of System V.

Organization of Driver Reference Manuals

Driver reference manual pages are similar to those in the *Programmer's Reference Manual*, with the page name followed by a section number in parentheses. All driver reference manual entries begin with a "D" to distinguish them as driver reference pages.

Currently, the reference pages for the different interfaces are published in separate volumes. Each manual contains three sections:

- D2 driver entry points
- D3 kernel functions used by drivers
- D4 system data structures accessed by drivers

Each section number is suffixed with a letter indicating the interfaces covered. The suffixes used are:

- D   Device Driver Interface (DDI)
- K   Driver-Kernel Interface (DKI)
- DK   DDI and DKI
- I   SCSI Device Interface (SDI)
- P   Portable Device Interface (PDI)
- X   Block and Character Interface (BCI)

For example, open(D2DK) refers to the open entry point routine for a driver, not to the open(2) system call documented in the *Programmer's Reference Manual*.

Conventions Used in This Document

Table 1-2 lists the textual conventions used in this book.

Table 1-2: Textual Conventions Used in This Book

Item	Style	Example
C Reserved Words	Constant Width	typedef
C typedef Declarations	Constant Width	caddr_t
Driver Routines	Constant Width	open routine
Error Values	Constant Width	EINTR
File Names	Constant Width	sys/conf.h
Flag Names	Constant Width	B_WRITE
Kernel Macros	Constant Width	minor
Kernel Functions	Constant Width	ttopen
Kernel Function Arguments	*Italics*	*bp*
Structure Members	Constant Width	b_addr
Structure Names	Constant Width	buf structure
Symbolic Constants	Constant Width	NULL
System Calls	Constant Width	ioctl(2)
C Library Calls	Constant Width	printf(3S)
Shell Commands	Constant Width	layers(1)
User-Defined Variable	*Italics*	*prefix*close

Related Learning Materials

AT&T provides a number of documents and courses to support users of our systems. For a listing see:

AT&T Computer Systems Documentation Catalog (300-000)
AT&T Computer Systems Education Catalog (300-002)

Documentation

Most documents listed here are available from the AT&T Customer Information Center. Refer to the six-digit select code (in parentheses, following the document title) when ordering.

If ordering by telephone, use the following numbers:

1-800-432-6600 (toll free within the continental United States)
1-317-352-8557 (outside the continental United States)

In addition to AT&T documents, the following list includes some commercially available documents that are relevant.

Driver Development

The UNIX *System V and V/386, Release 3, Block and Character Interface (BCI) Development Guide* (307-191) discusses driver development concepts, debugging, performance, installation, and other related driver topics for UNIX System V Release 3.

The UNIX *System V and V/386, Release 3, Block and Character Interface (BCI) Driver Reference Manual* (307-192) includes UNIX System V Rlease 3 reference material to be used in conjunction with the above manual. It describes driver entry point routines (Section D2X), kernel-level functions used in BCI drivers (Section D3X), and data structures accessed by BCI drivers (Section D4X).

The UNIX *System V PDI Driver Design Reference Manual* (305-014) defines the kernel functions and data structures used for Portable Driver Interface (PDI) drivers.

The UNIX *System V SCSI Driver Interface (SDI), Driver Design Reference Manual* (305-009) defines the kernel functions and data structures used for SDI drivers.

Related Learning Materials

STREAMS

The *Programmer's Guide: STREAMS* tells how to write drivers and access devices that use the STREAMS driver interface for character access.

C Programming Language and General Programming

Bentley, Jon Louis, *Writing Efficient Programs* (320-004), Englewood Cliffs, New Jersey: Prentice-Hall, 1982, gives hints for coding practices that improve process performance. Many of these ideas can be applied to driver code.

Kernighan, B. and D. Ritchie, *C Programming Language, Second Edition* (307-136), Englewood Cliffs, New Jersey: Prentice-Hall, 1988, defines the functions, structures, and interfaces of the C Programming Language. A short tutorial is included.

Lapin, J. E., *Portable C and UNIX System Programming*, Englewood Cliffs, New Jersey: Prentice-Hall, 1987, discusses how to maximize the portability of C language programs.

The *Programmer's Guide: Networking Interfaces* provides detailed information, with examples, on the Section 3N library that comprises the UNIX system Transport Level Interface (TLI).

The *Programmer's Guide: ANSI C and Programming Support Tools* includes instructions on using a number of UNIX utilities, including make and SCCS.

Assembly Language

The *AT&T 3B2/3B5/3B15 Computers Assembly Language Programming Manual* (305-000) describes the Assembly Language instructions used by AT&T 3B2, 3B15 and 3B4000 computers.

WE 32100 Microprocessor Information Manual, Maxicomputing in Microspace (307-730) introduces the WE 32100 microprocessor and summarizes its available support products.

Operating System

Bach, Maurice J., *Design of the UNIX Operating System* (320-044), Englewood Cliffs, New Jersey: Prentice-Hall, 1986, discusses the internals of the UNIX operating system, and includes an explanation of how drivers relate to the rest of the kernel.

The UNIX System V reference manuals are the standard reference materials for the UNIX operating system. This information is organized into three books, published separately for each system:

- The *System Administrator's Reference Manual* includes information on administrative commands (Section 1M), special device files (Section 7), and system-specific maintenance commands (Section 8).

- The *Programmer's Reference Manual* includes information on programming commands (Section 1), system calls (Section 2), library routines (Section 3), file formats (Section 4), and miscellaneous topics (Section 5).

- The *User's Reference Manual* includes information on UNIX system user-level commands (Section 1).

Software Packaging

The *Programmer's Guide: System Services and Application Packaging Tools* describes how to write the scripts necessary to install a driver (or other software) under the System Administration utility.

Training

The following courses are of particular interest to driver writers. To register for a class:

- Within the continental United States, call 1-800-TRAINER.
- Within Canada, call 1-800-221-1647.
- Outside the continental United States, call 1-201-953-7554.

Related Learning Materials

C Language for Experienced Programmers (UC1001) is a thorough, formal introduction to the C Programming Language.

Internal UNIX System Calls and Libraries Using C Language (UC1011) is an introduction to UNIX application programming in C. Topics include the execution environment, memory management, input/output, record and file locking, process generation, and interprocess communication (IPC).

UNIX System V Release 4 Device Drivers (UC1056) explores device driver mechanisms, operating system supplied functions, device driver source code examples, installation procedures and debugging techniques. Character, STREAMS, and block devices are covered as well as the entire I/O subsystem.

UNIX System V Release 4 Internals (UC1057) presents an in-depth look at UNIX System V, Release 4, including the process, file and I/O subsystems. New UNIX System V Release 4 concepts such as Network File Sharing (NFS), fast file system, and virtual file systems (VFS) are also reviewed.

Internal System Calls and Libraries (Part 1) (UC1058) presents the C language programmer's interface to UNIX System V Release 4. This course covers those system calls and library functions not pertaining to interprocess communication. Interprocess communication system calls and library functions are covered in Part 2 of this course.

Internal System Calls and Libraries (Part 2) (UC1059) presents UNIX System V Release 4 system calls and library functions pertaining to interprocess communication.

2. DRIVER ENTRY POINTS (D2)

2. DRIVER ENTRY POINTS (D2)

2 Driver Entry Points (D2)

Introduction 2-1

Overview of Driver Entry-Point Routines and Naming Conventions 2-2

Manual Pages 2-4
chpoll(D2DK) 2-4
close(D2DK) 2-6
init(D2D) 2-9
int(D2D) 2-10
ioctl(D2DK) 2-12
mmap(D2K) 2-16
open(D2DK) 2-17
print(D2DK) 2-19
put(D2DK) 2-20
read(D2DK) 2-22
segmap(D2K) 2-23
size(D2D) 2-25
srv(D2DK) 2-26
start(D2D) 2-28
strategy(D2DK) 2-29
write(D2DK) 2-30

Introduction

This chapter describes the DDI/DKI, DDI-only, and DKI-only entry-point routines a developer may include in a device driver. These are called entry-point routines because they provide the calling and return syntax from the kernel into the driver. For all driver types, these routines are called in response to system calls, when the computer is started, when a device generates an interrupt, or for STREAMS drivers, in response to STREAMS events.

All driver routines common to both DDI and DKI are identified with the (D2DK) cross reference code. All DDI-only or DKI-only routines are identified with the (D2D) or (D2K) reference codes respectively.

Functions provided to allow the driver to communicate with the kernel are described in section 3, and use the (D3DK), (D3D), and (D3K) cross reference codes.

In this section, reference pages contain the following headings:

- NAME describes the routine's purpose.
- SYNOPSIS summarizes the routine's calling and return syntax.
- ARGUMENTS describes each of the routine's arguments.
- DESCRIPTION provides general information about the routine.
- DEPENDENCIES lists possible dependent routine conditions.
- SEE ALSO gives sources for further information.

Overview of Driver Entry-Point Routines and Naming Conventions

Each driver is organized into two parts: the base level and the interrupt level. The base level interacts with the kernel and the user program; the interrupt level interacts with the device.

To uniquely identify a driver, a prefix string is added to the driver routine names. The prefix is defined in the driver's master file. For a driver with the *pre* prefix, the driver code may contain routines named *pre_open*, *pre_close*, *pre_init*, *pre_int*, and so forth. All global variables associated with the driver should also use the same prefix.

System routines can call subroutines that are assigned names by the driver writer. Subroutines should be declared as `static`, and should also use the driver prefix to increase code readability.

Table 2-1 summarizes the STREAMS driver entry points described in this section. These entry points may be used in either DDI or DKI.

Table 2-1: STREAMS Driver Entry Point Summary

Routine	Description
put	receive messages from the preceding queue
srv	service queued messages

Overview of Driver Entry-Point Routines and Naming Conventions

Table 2-2 summarizes the block I/O driver entry points described in this section. These entry points may be used in either DDI or DKI, except as noted.

Table 2-2: Driver Entry Points not Specific to STREAMS

Routine	Description	Type
chpoll	poll entry point for a non-STREAMS character driver	
close	relinquish access to a device	
init	initialize a device	DDI only
int	process a device interrupt	DDI only
ioctl	control a character device	
mmap	return page frame number	DKI only
open	gain access to a device	
print	display a driver message on system console	
read	read data from a device	
segmap	map device memory into user space	DKI only
size	return size of logical device	DDI only
start	start access to a device	DDI only
strategy	perform block I/O	
write	write data to a device	

chpoll (D2DK)

NAME
chpoll − poll entry point for a non-STREAMS character driver

SYNOPSIS
```
#include <sys/poll.h>
```
chpoll(dev_t *dev*, short *events*, int *anyyet*, short **reventsp*,
    struct pollhead ***phpp*);

ARGUMENTS
dev   The device number for the device to be polled.

events   The events that may occur. Valid events are:

POLLIN	Data are available to be read.
POLLOUT	Data may be written without blocking.
POLLPRI	High priority data may be read.
POLLHUP	A device hangup.
POLLERR	A device error.

anyyet   A flag that is non-zero if any other file descriptors in the `pollfd` array have events pending. The `poll(2)` system call takes a pointer to an array of `pollfd` structures as one of its arguments. See the `poll(2)` reference page for more details.

reventsp   A pointer to a bitmask of the returned events satisfied.

phpp   A pointer to a pointer to a `pollhead` structure. The `pollhead` structure is defined in `sys/poll.h`.

DESCRIPTION
The `chpoll` entry point routine is used by non-STREAMS character device drivers that wish to support polling. The driver must implement the polling discipline itself. The following rules must be followed when implementing the polling discipline:

1. Implement the following algorithm when the `chpoll` entry point is called:
```
if (events_are_satisfied_now) {
    *reventsp = mask_of_satisfied_events;
} else {
    *reventsp = 0;
    if (!anyyet)
        *phpp = &my_local_pollhead_structure;
}
return (0);
```

2. Allocate an instance of the `pollhead` structure. This instance may be tied to the per-minor data structure defined by the driver. The `pollhead` structure should be treated as a "black box" by the driver. None of its fields should be referenced. However, the size of this structure is guaranteed to remain the same across releases.

3. Call the `pollwakeup(D3DK)` function whenever an event of type `events` listed above occur. This function should only be called with one event at a time.

RETURN
    A `chpoll` routine should return 0 for success, or the appropriate error number.

SEE ALSO
    `pollwakeup`(D3DK), `poll`(2)

close (D2DK)

NAME
close – relinquish access to a device

SYNOPSIS [Block and Character]
```
#include <sys/types.h>
#include <sys/file.h>
#include <sys/errno.h>
#include <sys/open.h>
#include <sys/cred.h>
#include <sys/ddi.h>
```

int *prefix*close(dev_t *dev*, int *flag*, int *otyp*, cred_t **cred_p*);

ARGUMENTS

dev Device number.

flag File status flag, as set by the open(2) or modified by the fcntl(2) system calls. The flag is for information only—the file should always be closed completely. The flag is taken from the f_flag member of the file structure which is in file.h. Possible values are: FEXCL, FNDELAY, FREAD, and FWRITE. Refer to open(D2D) for more information.

otyp Parameter supplied so that the driver can determine how many times a device was opened and for what reasons. The flags assume the open routine may be called many times, but the close routine should only be called on the last close of a device.

  OTYP_BLK   close was through block interface for the device

  OTYP_CHAR close was through the raw/character interface for the device

  OTYP_MNT   close was called as a result of a umount(2) system call; unmount the file system associated with the block device

  OTYP_SWP   close a swapping device

  OTYP_LYR   close a layered process (a higher-level driver called the close routine of the device)

*cred_p Pointer to the cred(D4D) user credential structure.

SYNOPSIS [STREAMS]
```
#include <sys/types.h>
#include <sys/stream.h>
#include <sys/file.h>
#include <sys/errno.h>
#include <sys/open.h>
#include <sys/cred.h>
#include <sys/ddi.h>
```

int *prefix*close(queue_t **q*, int *flag*, cred_t **cred_p*);

close (D2DK)

ARGUMENTS

*q Pointer to `queue` structure used to reference the read side of the driver. (A queue is the central node of a collection of structures and routines pointed to by a queue.)

flag File status flag.

cred_p Pointer to the `cred(D4DK)` user credential structure.

DESCRIPTION

For STREAMS drivers, the `close` routine is called by the kernel through the `cdevsw` table entry for the device. (Modules use the `fmodsw` table.) A non-null value in the `d_str` field of the `cdevsw` entry points to a `streamtab` structure, which points to a `qinit` structure containing a pointer to the `close` routine. Non-STREAMS `close` routines are called directly from the `bdevsw` (block) or `cdevsw` (character) tables.

The `close` routine ends the connection between the user process and the device, and prepares the device (hardware and software) so that it is ready to be opened again.

A device may be opened simultaneously by multiple processes and the open driver routine is called for each open, but the kernel will only call the `close` routine when the last process using the device issues a `close`(2) or `umount`(2) system call or exits. (An exception is a close occurring with the *otyp* argument set to `OTYP_LYR`, for which a close (also having *otyp* = `OTYP_LYR`) occurs for each open.)

In general, a `close` routine should always check the validity of the minor number component of the *dev* parameter. The routine should also check permissions as necessary, by using the `cred(D4D)` structure (if pertinent), and the appropriateness of the *flag* and *otyp* parameter values.

A `close` routine could perform any of the following general functions:

> disable interrupts
> hang up phone lines
> rewind a tape
> deallocate buffers from a private buffering scheme
> unlock an unsharable device (that was locked in the open routine)
> flush buffers
> notify a device of the close
> deallocate any resources allocated on open

The `close` routines of STREAMS drivers and modules are called when a stream is dismantled or a module popped. The steps for dismantling a stream are performed in the following order. First, any multiplexor links present are unlinked and the lower streams are closed. Next, the following steps are performed for each module or driver on the stream, starting at the head and working toward the tail:

1. The write queue is given a chance to drain.

close (D2DK)

2. The `close` routine is called.
3. The module or driver is removed from the stream.

RETURN VALUE

The `close` routine should return 0 for success, or the appropriate error number. Refer to Appendix A for a list of DDI/DKI error numbers. Return errors rarely occur, but if a failure is detected, the driver should decide whether the severity of the problem warrants either displaying a message on the console or, in worst cases, triggering a system panic. Generally, a failure in a `close` routine occurs because a problem occurred in the associated device.

SEE ALSO

open(D2D), cred(D4DK)

NAME
init – initialize a device

SYNOPSIS
void *prefix*init();

DESCRIPTION
init and **start**(D2D) routines are used to initialize drivers and the devices they control. init routines are executed during system initialization, and can be used in drivers that do not require low level system services in order to be initialized. **start** routines are executed after low level services are enabled, such as interrupts and lower level kernel interfaces, but before file systems are available. Most drivers can use either an init or a **start** routine, or they can be used in combination. However, an init routine must be used in any driver controlling a device required to bring the system up.

Not all drivers need an init or a **start** routine. However, a driver must have either an init or **start** routine if it needs to allocate any data structures.

init and **start** routines can perform functions such as:

    allocating buffers for private buffering schemes

    mapping a device into virtual address space

    initializing hardware (for example, system generation or resetting the board)

    initializing a serial device in a character driver

Because the init and **start** routines are executed before there is user context, no functions that require user-context, such as **sleep**(D3DK), may be called.

SEE ALSO
start(D2D)

NAME

int – process a device interrupt

SYNOPSIS

void *prefix*int (int *ivec*) ;

ARGUMENT

ivec   Number used by the operating system to associate a driver's interrupt handler with an interrupting device. The makeup and interpretation of *ivec* is specific to each system implementation. In some systems, this number may be the logical device number, or a combination of logical device and logical controller numbers, used to map the correct interrupt routine with a subdevice. In others, this number could be the interrupt vector number.

DESCRIPTION

The int routine is the interrupt handler for both block and character hardware drivers. The interrupt handler is responsible for determining the reason for an interrupt, servicing the interrupt, and waking up any base-level driver processes sleeping on the interrupt completion. For example, when a disk drive has transfered information to the host to satisfy a read request, the disk drive's controller generates an interrupt. The CPU acknowledges the interrupt and calls the interrupt handler associated with that controller and disk drive. The interrupt routine services the interrupt and then wakes up the driver base-level process waiting for data. The base-level portion of the driver then conveys the data to the user.

In general, most interrupt routines must do the following tasks:

keep a record of interrupt occurrences

return immediately if no devices controlled by a driver caused the interrupt (only for systems supporting shared interrupts)

interpret the interrupt routine argument *ivec*

reject requests for devices that are not served by the device's controller

process interrupts that happen without cause (called spurious interrupts)

handle all possible device errors

wake processes that are sleeping on the resolution of an interrupt request

There are also many tasks the int routine must perform that are driver-type and device specific. For example, the following types of drivers require different functions from their int routines:

A block driver dequeues requests, wakes up processes sleeping on an I/O request, and ensures that system generation has completed.

A terminal driver receives and sends characters.

A printer driver ensures that characters are sent.

In addition, the functions of an int routine are device dependent. You should know the exact chip set that produces the interrupt for your device. You need to know the exact bit patterns of the device's control and status register and how data is transmitted into and out of your computer. These specifics differ for every device you access.

The `int` routine for an intelligent controller that does not use individual interrupt vectors for each subdevice must access the completion queue to determine which subdevice generated the interrupt. It must also update the status information, set/clear flags, set/clear error indicators, and so forth to complete the handling of a job. The code should also be able to handle a spurious completion interrupt identified by an empty completion queue. When the routine finishes, it should advance the unload pointer to the next entry in the completion queue.

If the driver called `biowait`(D3DK) or `sleep`(D3DK) to await the completion of an operation, the `int` routine must call `biodone`(D3DK) or `wakeup`(D3DK) to signal the process to resume.

`int` is only used with hardware drivers, not software drivers.

CAUTION: The `int` routine must never:

- contain calls to the `sleep` kernel function
- use functions that call `sleep`
- drop the interrupt priority level below the level at which the interrupt routine was entered
- call any function or routine that requires user context (that is, if it accesses or alters information associated with the running process)

NOTE: uiomove(D3DK) cannot be used in an interrupt routine when the uio_segflg member of the uio(D4DK) structure is set to UIO_USERSPACE (indicating a transfer between user and kernel space).

SEE ALSO

`biowait`(D3DK), `sleep`(D3DK), `biodone`(D3DK), `wakeup`(D3DK)

NAME

ioctl – control a character device

SYNOPSIS

```
#include <sys/cred.h>
#include <sys/types.h>
#include <sys/errno.h>
```

int *prefix*ioctl(dev_t *dev*, int *cmd*, int *arg*, int *mode*, cred_t **cred_p*,
    int **rval_p*);

ARGUMENTS

dev   Device number.

cmd   Command argument the driver ioctl routine interprets as the operation to be performed. It should be defined, along with an integer value that is actually passed, in the header file.

The I/O control command name and value can be defined in the driver code itself, but this is not recommended. If I/O control commands are defined in a header file, the user program and the driver can both access the same definitions to ensure that they agree about what each I/O control command value represents.

The I/O control command name is traditionally an all uppercase alphabetic string. This alphabetic name can be a mnemonic. You should try to keep the values for your I/O control commands distinct from others on the system. Each driver's I/O control commands are discrete, but it is possible for user-level code to access a driver with an I/O control command that is intended for another driver, which can lead to serious consequences, such as if it meant to pass "drop carrier on a communication line," but instead sends the argument to a disk where it is interpreted as "reformat drive." Permissions can be set to prevent most such events, but the more unique your I/O control command values are, the safer you are.

A number of different schemes are legal for assigning values to I/O control command names. The most straightforward is to use decimal numbers; for example

```
#define COMMAND1    01
#define COMMAND2    02
```

Similarly, one can assign hexadecimal numbers as values

```
#define COMMANDA    0x0a
#define COMMANDFF   0xff
```

The drawback to these methods is that one quickly gets an operating system that contains several instances of each I/O control command value, with the inherent risks discussed above.

A common method to assign I/O control command values that are less apt to be duplicated is to use a left-shifted 8 scheme. For instance

ioctl (D2DK)

```
#define COMMAND10    ('Q'<<8|10)
#define COMMAND11    ('Q'<<8|11)
#define COMMAND12    ('Q'<<8|12)
```

Alternately, the shift-left-8 scheme can be defined as a constant then used for the I/O control command definitions. For example

```
#define ROTA         ('q'<<8)
#define COMMAND23    (ROTA|234)
#define COMMAND25    (ROTA|254)
```

An alternative coding style is to use enumerations for the command argument, which allows the compiler to do additional type checking.

```
typedef enum {
    XX_COMMAND10 = 'Q'<<8 | 10,
    XX_COMMAND11 = 'Q'<<8 | 11,
    XX_COMMAND12 = 'Q'<<8 | 12,
} xx_cmds_t; ;
```

termio(7) specifies the command types that must work for AT&T terminal drivers. Terminal drivers typically have a command to read the current ioctl settings and at least one other that defines new settings.

arg Passes parameters between a user program and the driver.

When used with terminals, the argument is the address of a user program structure containing driver or hardware settings. Alternatively, the argument may be an integer that has meaning only to the driver. The interpretation of the argument is driver dependent and usually depends on the command type; the kernel does not interpret the argument.

mode Contains values set when the device was opened.

Use of this mode is optional. However, the driver may use it to determine if the device was opened for reading or writing. The driver makes this determination by checking the FREAD or FWRITE setting (values are in file.h).

See the *flag* argument description of the open routine for further values for the ioctl routine's *mode* argument.

*cred_p Pointer to the cred(D4DK) user credential structure.

*rval_p Pointer to return value for calling process. The driver may elect to set the value which is valid only if the ioctl(D2DK) succeeds.

DESCRIPTION

The ioctl(D2DK) routine provides character-access drivers with an alternate entry point that can be used for almost any operation other than a simple transfer of characters in and out of buffers. Most often, ioctl is used to control device hardware parameters and establish the protocol used by the driver in processing data.

ioctl (D2DK)

The kernel looks up the device's file table entry, determines that this is a character device, and looks up the entry point routines in `cdevsw`. The kernel then packages the user request and arguments as integers and passes them to the driver's `ioctl` routine. The kernel itself does no processing of the passed command, so it is up to the user program and the driver to agree on what the arguments mean.

I/O control commands are used to implement the terminal settings passed from `ttymon(1M)` and `stty(1)`, to format disk devices, to implement a trace driver for debugging, and to clean up character queues. Since the kernel does not interpret the command type that defines the operation, a driver is free to define its own commands.

Drivers that use an `ioctl` routine typically have a command to "read" the current `ioctl` settings, and at least one other that sets new settings. You can use the mode argument to determine if the device unit was opened for reading or writing, if necessary, by checking the `FREAD` or `FWRITE` setting.

If the third argument, *arg*, is a pointer to user space, the driver should call the `copyin(D3DK)` and `copyout(D3DK)` functions to transfer data between kernel and user space.

To implement I/O control commands for a driver the following two steps are required:

1. Define the I/O control command names and the associated value in the driver's header file and comment the commands.
2. Code the `ioctl` routine in the driver that defines the functionality for each I/O control command name that is in the header file.

The `ioctl` routine is coded with instructions on the proper action to take for each command. It is basically a `switch` statement, with each `case` definition corresponding to an `ioctl` name to identify the action that should be taken. However, the command passed to the driver by the user process is an integer value associated with the command name in the header file.

It is critical that command definitions and routines be clearly commented. Because there is so much flexibility in how commands are used, uncommented commands can be very difficult to interpret at a later time.

Terminal drivers use and support the `ioctl` commands defined on the `termio(7)` manual page. For instance, `TCGETA` gets the parameters associated with the terminal and stores them in the structure referenced in the third argument of the routine call. `TCSETA` sets the parameters associated with the terminal from the structure referenced in the third argument.

NOTE: STREAMS drivers do not have `ioctl` routines. The stream head converts I/O control commands to `M_IOCTL` messages, which are handled by the driver's `put(D2DK)` or `srv(D2DK)` routine.

RETURN VALUE

The `ioctl` routine should return 0 for success, or the appropriate error number. Refer to Appendix A for a list of DDI/DKI error numbers. The driver may also set the value returned to the calling process through the *rval_p* pointer.

SEE ALSO

copyin(D3DK), copyout(D3DK)

mmap(D2K)   mmap(D2K)

NAME
    mmap – check virtual mapping for memory mapped device

SYNOPSIS
```
#include <sys/types.h>
#include <sys/cred.h>
#include <sys/mman.h>
#include <sys/vm.h>
```
    int *prefix*mmap(dev_t *dev*, off_t *off*, int *prot*);

ARGUMENTS
    dev   Device whose memory is to be mapped.

    off   Offset within device memory at which mapping begins.

    prot   Protection flag from mman.h (e.g., PROT_WRITE, PROT_READ).

DESCRIPTION
    The **mmap** entry point is a required entry point for character drivers supporting memory-mapped devices. A memory mapped device has memory that can be mapped into a process's address space. The **mmap**(2) system call, when applied to a character special file, allows this device memory to be mapped into user space for direct access by the user application (no kernel buffering overhead is required).

    An **mmap**(D2K) routine checks if each offset is within the range of pages supported by the device. For example, a device that has 512 bytes of memory that can be mapped into user space should not support offsets greater than 512. If the offset does not exist, then −1 is returned. If the offset does exist, **mmap** returns the masked page table entry for the page at offset *off* in the device's memory.

    mmap should only be supported for memory-mapped devices or pseudo-devices. See the **segmap**(D2K) reference page for further information on memory-mapped device drivers.

RETURN VALUE
    If the protection and offset are valid for the device, the driver should return the masked page table entry, typically obtained using the function hat_getkpfnum(D3K), for the page at offset *off* in the device's memory. If not, −1 should be returned.

SEE ALSO
    segmap(D2K), hat_getkpfnum(D3K)

open (D2DK)

NAME
open – gain access to a device

SYNOPSIS [Block and Character]
```
#include <sys/types.h>
#include <sys/file.h>
#include <sys/errno.h>
#include <sys/open.h>
#include <sys/cred.h>
```
*prefix*open(dev_t **dev*, int *flag*, int *otyp*, cred_t **cred_p*);

ARGUMENTS

dev Pointer to a device number.

flag Information passed from the user program open(2) or create(2) system call instructs the driver on how to open the file. The bit settings for the flag are found in file.h associated with the f_flag member of the file structure. Valid settings are:

   FNDELAY open the device and return immediately without sleeping (do not block the open even if there is a problem)

   FREAD open the device with read-only permission (if ORed with FWRITE, then allow both read and write access)

   FWRITE open a device with write-only permission (if ORed with FREAD, then allow both read and write access)

otyp Parameter supplied so that the driver can determine how many times a device was opened and for what reasons. The flags assume the open routine may be called many times, but the close routine should only be called on the last close of a device. All flags are defined in open.h.

   OTYP_BLK open occurred through block interface for the device

   OTYP_CHAR open occurred through the raw/character interface for the device

   OTYP_MNT the file system on the block device is being opened due to a mount(2) system call

   OTYP_SWP open a swapping device

   OTYP_LYR open a layered process. This flag is used when one driver calls another driver's open or close routine. In this case, there is exactly one close for each open called. This permits software drivers to exist above hardware drivers and removes any ambiguity from the hardware driver regarding how a device is used. This flag applies to both block and character devices.

*cred_p Pointer to the cred(D4DK) user credential structure.

open (D2DK)

SYNOPSIS [STREAMS]

```
#include <sys/file.h>
#include <sys/stream.h>
```

*prefix*open (queue_t *q, dev_t *dev, int *oflag*, int *sflag*, cred_t *$cred\_p$);

ARGUMENTS [STREAMS]

q A pointer to the read queue. (A queue is the central node of a collection of structures and routines pointed to by a queue.)

dev Pointer to a device number. For modules, *dev* always points to the device number associated with the driver at the end (tail) of the stream.

oflag Valid *oflag* values are the same as those listed above, with the exception that FAPPEND, FCREAT, and FTRUNC have no meaning to a STREAMS device. For modules, *oflag* is always set to 0.

sflag Valid values are as follows:

CLONEOPEN Eliminates the need for user processes to poll many minor devices when looking for an unused one. If the driver wishes to assign the device a device file, the open routine must assign and return a minor number. If no device file is required, the open routine does not have to return a minor number.

MODOPEN Indicates that an open routine is being called for a module, not a driver. Drivers should return error numbers or 0 if an open is attempted with *sflag* set to MODOPEN.

0 Indicates a driver opened directly, without calling the clone driver.

$cred\_p$ Pointer to the cred(D4DK) user credential structure.

DESCRIPTION

The driver's open routine is called by the kernel through the cdevsw or bdevsw entry for the device during an open(2) or a mount(2) on the special file for the device. The routine should verify that the minor number component of *dev* is valid, that the type of access requested by *otyp* and *flag* is appropriate for the device, and, if required, check permissions using the user credentials pointed to by *$cred\_p$*.

RETURN VALUE

The open routine should return 0 for success, or the appropriate error number. Refer to Appendix A for a list of DDI/DKI error numbers.

SEE ALSO

close(D2DK)

print (D2DK)　　　　　　　　　　　　　　　　　　　　　　　　　　　　　**print (D2DK)**

NAME
print – display a driver message on system console

SYNOPSIS
```
#include <sys/types.h>
#include <sys/errno.h>

int prefixprint(dev_t dev, char *str);
```

ARGUMENTS
dev　　　　Device number.

*str　　　　Pointer to a character string describing the problem. An explanation of the problem contained in the string should be included in the driver output.

DESCRIPTION
The `print` routine is called indirectly by the kernel through the `bdevsw` entry for the device when the kernel has detected an exceptional condition (such as out of space) in the device. To display the message on the console, the driver should use the `cmn_err`(D3DK) kernel function.

RETURN VALUE
The `print` routine should return 0 for success, or the appropriate error number. Refer to Appendix A for a list of DDI/DKI error numbers. The `print` routine can fail if the driver implemented a non-standard `print` routine that attempted to perform error logging, but was unable to complete the logging for whatever reason. Generally, since most `print` routines call the `cmn_err`(D3DK) function, and this function is declared as `void`, return values are seldom returned from this routine. If a failure occurs, call `cmn_err` to display a message to the operator.

SEE ALSO
cmn_err(D3DK)

put (D2DK)

NAME
put – receive messages from the preceding queue

SYNOPSIS
```
#include <sys/types.h>
#include <sys/stream.h>
#include <sys/stropts.h>
```
void *prefix*rput(queue_t *q, mblk_t *mp);   /* read side */

void *prefix*wput(queue_t *q, mblk_t *mp);   /* write side */

ARGUMENTS
*q Pointer to the queue(D4DK) structure.

mp Pointer to the message block.

DESCRIPTION
The primary task of the put routine is to coordinate the passing of messages from one queue to the next in a stream. The put routine is called by the preceding stream component (module, driver, or stream head). put routines are designated "write" or "read" depending on the direction of message flow.

With few exceptions, a module or driver must have a put routine. One exception is the read side of a driver, which does not need a put routine because there is no component downstream to call it. The put routine is always called before the component's corresponding srv(D2DK) (service) routine, and so put should be used for the immediate processing of messages.

A put routine must do at least one of the following when it receives a message:

 pass the message to the next component on the stream by calling the putnext(D3DK) function

 process the message, if immediate processing is required (for example, high priority messages)

 enqueue the message (with the putq(D3DK) function) for deferred processing by the service srv(D2DK) routine

Typically, a put routine will switch on message type, which is contained in the db_type member of the datab structure pointed to by *mp*. The action taken by the put routine depends on the message type. For example, a put routine might process high priority messages, enqueue normal messages, and handle an unrecognized message by changing its type to M_IOCNAK (negative acknowledgement) and sending it back to the stream head using the qreply(D3DK) function.

The putq(D3DK) function can be used as a module's put routine when no special processing is required and all messages are to be enqueued for the srv routine.

put routines do not have user context and so may not call sleep(D3DK).

SEE ALSO
The *BCI Driver Development Guide*, Chapter 7, "STREAMS"

put (D2DK)   **put (D2DK)**

The *STREAMS Programmer's Guide*

`streamtab`(D4DK), `putctl`(D3DK), `putctl1`(D3DK), `putnext`(D3DK), `putq`(D3DK), `qreply`(D3DK), `srv`(D2DK)

read (D2DK)

NAME
read – read data from a device

SYNOPSIS
```
#include <sys/types.h>
#include <sys/errno.h>
#include <sys/open.h>
#include <sys/uio.h>
#include <sys/cred.h>
```

*prefix*read(dev_t *dev,* uio **uio_p,* cred_t **cred_p*);

ARGUMENTS
dev
Device number.

*uio_p Pointer to the uio(D4DK) structure that describes where the data is to be stored in user space.

*cred_p Pointer to the cred(D4DK) user credential structure for the I/O transaction.

DESCRIPTION
The driver **read** routine is called indirectly through **cdevsw** by the read(2) system call. The **read** routine should check the validity of the minor number component of *dev* and the user credentials contained in the cred(D4DK) structure pointed to by **cred_p* (if pertinent). The **read** routine should supervise the data transfer into the user space described by the uio(D4DK) structure.

RETURN VALUE
The **read** routine should return 0 for success, or the appropriate error number. Refer to Appendix A for a list of error values.

SEE ALSO
write(D2DK)

segmap (D2K)

NAME
segmap – map device memory into user space

SYNOPSIS
```
#include <sys/types.h>
#include <sys/mman.h>
#include <sys/param.h>
#include <sys/vm.h>
```
int *prefix*segmap(dev_t *dev*, off_t *off*, struct as **asp*, addr_t **addrp*,
    off_t *len*, unsigned int *prot*, unsigned int *maxprot*,
    unsigned int *flags*, cred_t **cred_p*);

ARGUMENTS

dev Device whose memory is to be mapped.

off Offset within device memory at which mapping begins.

*asp Pointer to the address space into which the device memory should be mapped.

*addrp Pointer to the address in the address space to which the device memory should be mapped.

len Length (in bytes) of the memory to be mapped.

prot Protection flag (from `sys/mman.h`) for example, `PROT_WRITE`, `PROT_READ`, `PROT_USER` (indicating the mapping is being done as a result of a mmap(2) system call).

maxprot Maximum protection flag possible for attempted map (`PROT_WRITE` may be masked out if the user opened the special file read-only). If (`maxprot & prot`) != prot then there is an access violation.

flags Flags indicating type of mmap (for example, `MAP_SHARED` vs. `MAP_PRIVATE`), whether the user specified an address (`MAP_FIXED`). Found in `sys/mman.h`.

*cred_p Pointer to the `cred`(D4DK) user credentials structure.

DESCRIPTION

The `segmap` entry point is an optional routine for character drivers that support memory mapping. The mmap(2) system call, when applied to a character special file, allows device memory to be mapped into user space for direct access by the user application (no kernel buffering overhead is required).

Typically, a character driver that needs to support the mmap(2) system call supplies either a single mmap(D2K) entry point, or both an mmap and a segmap entry point routine (see the mmap(D2K) reference page). If no segmap entry point is provided for the driver, the default kernel segmap routine is called to perform the mapping.

A driver for a memory-mapped device would provide a segmap entry point if it:

> requires the mapping to be done through a virtual memory (VM) segment driver other than the default `seg_dev` driver provided by the kernel

segmap(D2K) segmap(D2K)

needs to control the selection of the user address at which the mapping occurs in the case where the user did not specify an address in the mmap(2) system call

Among the responsibilities of a **segmap** entry point are:

Select a segment driver and check the memory map flags for appropriateness to the segment driver. For example, the **seg_dev** segment driver does not support memory maps that are marked MAP_PRIVATE (copy-on-write).

Verify that the range to be mapped makes sense in the context of the device (does the offset and length make sense for the device memory that is to be mapped). Typically, this task is performed by calling the mmap(D2K) entry point.

If MAP_FIXED is not set in *flags*, obtain a user address at which to map. Otherwise, unmap any existing mappings at the user address specified.

Perform the mapping and return the error status if it fails.

RETURN VALUE

The routine returns 0 if the driver is successful in performing the memory map of its device address space into the specified address space. An error number should be returned on failure. For example, valid error numbers would be ENXIO if the offset/length pair specified exceeds the limits of the device memory, or EINVAL if the driver detects an invalid type of mapping attempted.

SEE ALSO

mmap(D2K)

size(D2D) size(D2D)

NAME
> size – return size of logical device

SYNOPSIS
> #include <sys/types.h>
>
> *prefix*size(dev_t *dev*);

ARGUMENT
> *dev*   The logical device number.

DESCRIPTION
> Returns the number of 512-byte units on a logical device (partition). Although this routine is not required, it is recommended that new drivers include one as the Release 4.0 kernel calls the size routine on behalf of certain UNIX commands such as stat(3G).

RETURN VALUE
> The number of 512 byte units on the logical device specified by *dev*, or −1 on failure.

srv (D2DK)

NAME
srv – service queued messages

SYNOPSIS
```
#include <sys/types.h>
#include <sys/stream.h>
#include <sys/stropts.h>
```
void *prefix*rsrv(queue_t *q*);   /* read side */

void *prefix*wsrv(queue_t *q*);   /* write side */

ARGUMENTS
q   Pointer to the queue(D4DK) structure

DESCRIPTION
The optional service (srv) routine may be included in a STREAMS module or driver for one or more of the following reasons:

> to provide greater control over the flow of messages in a stream
>
> to make it possible to defer the processing of some messages to avoid depleting system resources
>
> to combine small messages into larger ones, or break large messages into smaller ones
>
> to recover from resource allocation failure. A module's or driver's put(D3DK) routine can test for the availability of a resource, and if it is not available, enqueue the message for later processing by the srv routine.

A message is first passed to a module's or driver's put(D2DK) routine, which may or may not do some processing. It must then either

> pass the message to the next stream component with putnext(D3DK)
>
> if a srv routine has been included, it may call the putq(D3DK) function to place the message on the queue

Once a message has been enqueued, the STREAMS scheduler controls the calling of the service routine. Service routines are called in FIFO order by the scheduler. No guarantees can be made about how long it will take for a srv routine to be called except that it will happen before any user level process are run.

Every stream component (stream head, module or driver) has limit values it uses to implement flow control. Tunable high and low water marks are checked to stop and restart the flow of message processing. Flow control limits apply only between two adjacent components with srv routines.

STREAMS messages can be defined to have up to 256 different priorities to support some networking protocol requirements for multiple bands of data flow. At a minimum, a stream must distinguish between normal (priority zero) messages and high priority messages (such as M_IOCACK). High priority messages are always placed at the head of the srv routine's queue, after any other enqueued high priority messages. Next are messages from all included priority bands, which are enqueued in decreasing order of priority. Each priority band has its own flow control limits. If a flow controlled band is stopped, all lower priority bands are also stopped.

Once a `srv` routine is called by the STREAMS scheduler it must process all messages on its queue. The following steps are general guidelines for processing messages. Keep in mind that many of the details of how a `srv` routine should be written depend of the implementation, the direction of flow (upstream or downstream), and whether it is for a module or a driver.

1. Use the `getq`(D3DK) function to get the next enqueued message.
2. If the message is high priority, process (if appropriate) and pass to the next stream component with the `putnext`(D3DK) function.
3. If it is not a high priority message (and therefore subject to flow control), attempt to send it to the next stream component with a `srv` routine. Use `bcanput`(D3DK) to determine if this can be done.
4. If the message cannot be passed, put it back on the queue with `putbq`(D3DK). If it can be passed, process (if appropriate) and pass with `putnext`.

NOTE: Each stream module has a read and write service (`srv`) routine. If a service routine is not needed (because the `put` routine processes all messages), a `NULL` pointer should be placed in module's `qinit` structure. Do not use the `nulldev` routine instead of the `NULL` pointer. Use of `nulldev` for a `srv` routine may result in flow control errors.

SEE ALSO

The *BCI Driver Development Guide*, Chapter 7, "STREAMS"

The *STREAMS Programmer's Guide*, Chapter 5, "Messages"

`bcanput`(D3DK), `canput`(D3DK), `getq`(D3DK), `put`(D2DK), `putbq`(D3DK), `putnext`(D3DK), `putq`(D3DK), `queue`(D4DK)

NAME
start – start access to a device

SYNOPSIS
void *prefix*start();

DESCRIPTION
The start routine is called when a computer starts placing a device into a known state. At the time this routine is called, the developer cannot depend on root being mounted. However, the developer can depend on low level system services being available such as interrupts enabled.

A start routine may perform the following types of activities:

> initialize data structures for device access
>
> allocate buffers for private buffering scheme
>
> map device into virtual address space
>
> initialize hardware (for example, perform a system generation and reset the board)
>
> initialize the serial device for character drivers
>
> initialize any static data associated with the driver

SEE ALSO
init(D2DK)

strategy (D2DK)

NAME
strategy – perform block I/O

SYNOPSIS
```
#include <sys/types.h>
#include <sys/buf.h>

int prefixstrategy(struct buf *bp);
```

ARGUMENT
bp Pointer to the **buf(D4DK)** structure.

DESCRIPTION
The **strategy** routine is called indirectly (through **bdevsw**) by the kernel to read and write blocks of data on the block device. **strategy** may also be called directly or indirectly (via a call to the kernel function **physiock(D3D)**), to support the raw character interface of a block device (**read(D2DK)**, **write(D2DK)** and **ioctl(D2DK)**). The **strategy** routine's responsibility is to set up and initiate the transfer.

RETURN VALUE
On an error condition, OR the **b_flags** member of the **buf(D4DK)** structure with **B_ERROR** and set the **b_error** member to the appropriate error value.

SEE ALSO
read(D2DK), **write(D2DK)**

NAME

write – write data to a device

SYNOPSIS

```
#include <sys/types.h>
#include <sys/errno.h>
#include <sys/open.h>
#include <sys/cred.h>
```

int *prefix*write(dev_t *dev*, uio_t **uio_p*, cred_t **cred_p*);

ARGUMENTS

dev
Device number.

uio_p   Pointer to the uio(D4DK) structure that describes where the data is to be stored in user space.

cred_p Pointer to the cred(D4DK) user credential structure for the I/O transaction.

DESCRIPTION

Used for character or raw data I/O, the driver **write** routine is called indirectly through cdevsw by the **write**(2) system call. The **write** routine supervises the data transfer from user space to a device described by the uio(D4DK) structure.

The **write** routine should check the validity of the minor number component of *dev* and the user credentials pointed to by *cred_p* (if pertinent).

RETURN VALUE

The **write** routine should return 0 for success, or the appropriate error number. Refer to Appendix A for a list of DDI/DKI error numbers.

SEE ALSO

read(D2DK)

3. KERNEL FUNCTIONS (D3)

3. KERNEL FUNCTIONS (D3)

3 Kernel Functions (D3)

Introduction	3-1
Function Summary	3-2

Manual Pages	3-7
adjmsg(D3DK)	3-7
allocb(D3DK)	3-8
backq(D3DK)	3-10
bcanput(D3DK)	3-11
bcopy(D3DK)	3-12
biodone(D3DK)	3-14
biowait(D3DK)	3-16
bp_mapin(D3DK)	3-17
bp_mapout(D3DK)	3-18
brelse(D3DK)	3-19
btop(D3DK)	3-20
btopr(D3DK)	3-21
bufcall(D3DK)	3-22
bzero(D3DK)	3-24
canput(D3DK)	3-25
clrbuf(D3DK)	3-26
cmn_err(D3DK)	3-27
copyb(D3DK)	3-30
copyin(D3DK)	3-32
copymsg(D3DK)	3-33
copyout(D3DK)	3-35
datamsg(D3DK)	3-37
delay(D3DK)	3-38
dma_pageio(D3D)	3-40
drv_getparm(D3DK)	3-42
drv_hztousec(D3DK)	3-44

Table of Contents   i

Table of Contents

drv_priv(D3DK)	3-45
drv_usectohz(D3DK)	3-46
drv_usecwait(D3DK)	3-47
dupb(D3DK)	3-48
dupmsg(D3DK)	3-50
enableok(D3DK)	3-51
esballoc(D3DK)	3-52
esbbcall(D3DK)	3-53
etoimajor(D3D)	3-54
flushband(D3DK)	3-55
flushq(D3DK)	3-56
freeb(D3DK)	3-58
freemsg(D3DK)	3-59
freerbuf(D3DK)	3-60
getemajor(D3D)	3-61
geteminor(D3D)	3-62
geterror(D3DK)	3-63
getmajor(D3DK)	3-64
getminor(D3DK)	3-65
getq(D3DK)	3-66
getrbuf(D3DK)	3-67
getvec(D3D)	3-68
hat_getkpfnum(D3K)	3-69
hdeeqd(D3D)	3-70
hdelog(D3D)	3-73
insq(D3DK)	3-76
itoemajor(D3D)	3-78
kmem_alloc(D3DK)	3-79
kmem_free(D3DK)	3-80
kmem_zalloc(D3DK)	3-81
kvtophys(D3D)	3-82
linkb(D3DK)	3-83
makedevice(D3DK)	3-84
max(D3DK)	3-85
min(D3DK)	3-86
msgdsize(D3DK)	3-87
noenable(D3DK)	3-88

Table of Contents

OTHERQ(D3DK)	3-89
page_numtopp(D3DK)	3-90
page_pptonum(D3DK)	3-91
physiock(D3D)	3-92
pollwakeup(D3DK)	3-95
ptob(D3DK)	3-96
pullupmsg(D3DK)	3-97
putbq(D3DK)	3-99
putctl(D3DK)	3-100
putctl1(D3DK)	3-102
putnext(D3DK)	3-103
putq(D3DK)	3-104
qenable(D3DK)	3-105
qreply(D3DK)	3-106
qsize(D3DK)	3-108
RD(D3DK)	3-109
rmalloc(D3DK)	3-110
rmfree(D3DK)	3-114
rminit(D3DK)	3-115
rmsetwant(D3DK)	3-116
rmvb(D3DK)	3-117
rmvq(D3DK)	3-118
rmwant(D3DK)	3-120
SAMESTR(D3DK)	3-121
sleep(D3DK)	3-122
spl(D3D)	3-125
strlog(D3DK)	3-127
strqget(D3DK)	3-128
strqset(D3DK)	3-129
testb(D3DK)	3-130
timeout(D3DK)	3-132
uiomove(D3DK)	3-133
unlinkb(D3DK)	3-134
untimeout(D3DK)	3-135
ureadc(D3DK)	3-138
useracc(D3DK)	3-139
uwritec(D3DK)	3-140

Table of Contents

vtop(D3D)	3-141
wakeup(D3DK)	3-142
WR(D3DK)	3-143

Introduction

This chapter describes the kernel functions available for use by device drivers. Each function is described in a separate entry. Most functions are part of both DDI and DKI—these are indicated by the (D3DK) cross reference code. Functions belonging only to DDI are cross-referenced by (D3D) and DKI-only functions are marked (D3K).

In this section, the information for each driver function is organized under the following headings:

- NAME summarizes the function's purpose.

- SYNOPSIS shows the syntax of the function's entry point in the source code. #include statements are shown for required header files.

- ARGUMENTS describes any arguments required to invoke the function.

- DESCRIPTION describes general information about the function.

- RETURN VALUE describes the return values and messages that can result from invoking the function.

- LEVEL indicates from which driver level (base or interrupt) the function can be called.

- SEE ALSO indicates functions that are related by usage and sources, and which can be referred to for further information.

- EXAMPLE shows how the function can be used in driver code.

> **NOTE** The ddi.h header file undefines macros that have been reimplemented as functions in UNIX System V Release 4.0. Always place ddi.h at the end of the list of include statements to avoid contention between macro and function declarations.

Function Summary

Table 3-1 summarizes the STREAMS functions described in this section. STREAMS functions may be used in either DDI or DKI.

Table 3-1: STREAMS Kernel Function Summary

Routine	Description
adjmsg	remove the specified number of bytes from a message
allocb	allocate a message block
backq	get pointer to the previous queue
bcanput	test for flow control in specified priority band
bufcall	get buffer when allocb fails
canput	test for room in a message queue
copyb	copy a message block
copymsg	copy a message to a new message
datamsg	test whether a message is a data message
dupb	duplicate a message block descriptor
dupmsg	duplicate a message
enableok	enable a queue for service
esballoc	allocate a message block with a shared buffer
esbbcall	get message header when esballoc fails
flushband	flush messages for specified priority band
flushq	remove messages from a queue
freeb	free a message block
freemsg	free all message blocks in a message
getq	get a message from the front of a queue
insq	insert a message into a queue
linkb	concatenate two message blocks

Table 3-1: STREAMS Kernel Function Summary (continued)

Routine	Description
msgdsize	return the number of bytes in a message
noenable	prevent a queue from being scheduled
OTHERQ	get a pointer to a module's other queue
pullupmsg	concatenate bytes in a message
putbq	place a message at the head of a queue
putctl	put a control message on a queue
putctl1	put a control message with a one-byte parameter on a queue
putnext	send a message to the next module in the stream
putq	put a message on a queue
qenable	enable a queue
qreply	send a message in the reverse direction
qsize	find the number of messages on a queue
RD	get a pointer to a module's read queue
rmvb	remove a message block from a queue
rmvq	remove a message from a queue
SAMESTR	test if next queue is same type
strlog	submit messages for logging
strqget	get information about a queue
strqset	change information about a queue
testb	check for an available buffer
unlinkb	remove the message block from the head of a message
WR	get pointer to this module's write queue

Introduction

Table 3-2 summarizes the functions not specific to STREAMS. Functions can be used in either DDI or DKI, except as noted.

Table 3-2: Kernel Functions Not Specific to STREAMS

Routine	Description	Type
bcopy	copy data between locations in the kernel, for example, from one buffer to another	
biodone	release buffer after block I/O and wakeup processes	
biowait	suspend processes pending completion of block I/O	
bp_mapin	allocate virtual address space	
bp_mapout	deallocate virtual address space	
brelse	return buffer to the kernel	
btop	return number of memory pages contained in specified number of bytes (downward rounding)	
btopr	return number of memory pages contained in specified number of bytes (upward rounding)	
bzero	clear memory for a number of bytes	
clrbuf	erase buffer contents	
cmn_err	display message or panic the system	
copyin	copy data from user space to the driver	
copyout	copy data from the driver to user space	
delay	delay for specified number of clock ticks	
dma_pageio	break up DMA requests	DDI only
drv_getparm	retrieve kernel state information	
drv_hztousec	convert from clock ticks to microseconds	
drv_priv	determine driver privileges	
drv_usectohz	convert from microseconds to clock ticks	

Table 3-2: Kernel Functions Not Specific to STREAMS (continued)

Routine	Description	Type
`drv_usecwait`	wait for specified number of microseconds	
`etoimajor`	convert external major number to internal major number	DDI only
`freerbuf`	free a raw buffer header	
`getemajor`	get external major number	DDI only
`geteminor`	get external minor number	DDI only
`geterror`	return an I/O error	
`getmajor`	get major number	
`getminor`	get minor number	
`getrbuf`	get a raw buffer header	
`getvec`	get an interrupt vector for a given virtual board address	DDI only
`hat_getkpfnum`	get page frame number for address	DKI only
`hdeeqd`	initialize error logging in the hard disk	DDI only
`hdelog`	log a hard disk error	DDI only
`itoemajor`	convert internal major number to external number	DDI only
`kmem_alloc`	allocate storage from kernel free space	
`kmem_free`	free previously allocated kernel memory	
`kmem_zalloc`	allocate and clear storage from kernel free memory	
`kvtophys`	convert kernel virtual to physical address	DDI only
`makedevice`	create a device number	
`max`	return the larger of two integers	
`min`	return the smaller of two integers	
`page_numtopp`	convert page frame number to page structure	

Kernel Functions (D3)

Introduction

Table 3-2: Kernel Functions Not Specific to STREAMS (continued)

Routine	Description	Type
page_pptonum	convert page structure to page frame number	
physiock	validate and issue raw I/O request	DDI only
pollwakeup	inform a process that an event has occurred	
ptob	convert size in pages to size in bytes	
rmalloc	allocate space from a private space management map	
rmfree	free space back into a private space management map	
rminit	initialize a private space management map	
rmsetwant	set the map's wait flag for wakeup	
rmwant	wait for free memory	
sleep	suspend execution	
spl	suspend or allow interrupts	
timeout	call function in clock ticks	
uiomove	copy kernel data using uio structure	
untimeout	cancel timeout with matching ID	
ureadc	add character to uio structure	
useracc	verify user access to data structures	
uwritec	remove a character from a uio structure	
vtop	convert virtual to physical address	DDI only
wakeup	resume suspended execution	

adjmsg (D3DK)

NAME
adjmsg – trim bytes from a message

SYNOPSIS
```
#include <sys/stream.h>
```

int adjmsg(mblk_t *mp, int len);

ARGUMENTS
*mp   Pointer to the message to be trimmed.

len   The number of bytes to be removed.

DESCRIPTION
adjmsg removes bytes from a message. |len| (the absolute value of len) specifies how many bytes are to be removed. If len is greater than 0, bytes are removed from the head of the message. If len is less than 0, bytes are removed from the tail. adjmsg fails if |len| is greater than the number of bytes in mp.

RETURN VALUE
If the message can be trimmed successfully, 1 is returned. Otherwise, 0 is returned.

LEVEL
Base or Interrupt

SEE ALSO
BCI Driver Development Guide, Chapter 7, "STREAMS"

allocb (D3DK)

NAME

allocb – allocate a message block

SYNOPSIS

#include <sys/stream.h>

mblk_t *allocb(int *size*, int *pri*);

ARGUMENTS

size   The number of bytes in the message block.

pri   Priority of the request (no longer used).

DESCRIPTION

allocb tries to allocate a STREAMS message block. Buffer allocation fails only when the system is out of memory. If no buffer is available, the bufcall(D3DK) function can help a module recover from an allocation failure.

NOTE: The *pri* argument is no longer used in UNIX System V Release 4, but is retained for compatibility with existing drivers.

The following figure identifies the data structure members that are affected when a message block is allocated.

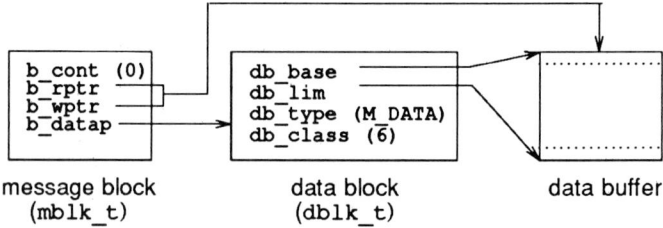

message block   data block   data buffer
(mblk_t)   (dblk_t)

RETURN VALUE

If successful, allocb returns a pointer to the allocated message block of type M_DATA (defined in sys/stream.h). If a block cannot be allocated, a NULL pointer is returned.

LEVEL

Base or Interrupt

SEE ALSO

BCI Driver Development Guide, Chapter 7, "STREAMS"

STREAMS Programmer's Guide, Chapter 5, "Messages"

bufcall(D3DK), esballoc(D3DK), esbbcall(D3DK), testb(D3DK)

EXAMPLE

Given a pointer to a queue (*q*) and an error number (*err*), the send_error routine sends an M_ERROR type message to the stream head.

If a message cannot be allocated, 0 is returned, indicating an allocation failure (line 8). Otherwise, the message type is set to M_ERROR (line 10). Line 11 increments the write pointer (bp->b_wptr) by the size (one byte) of the data in the message.

allocb (D3DK)

A message must be sent up the read side of the stream to arrive at the stream head. To determine whether *q* points to a read queue or a write queue, the `q->q_flag` member is tested to see if `QREADR` is set (line 13). If it is not set, *q* points to a write queue, and in line 14 the `RD`(D3DK) function is used to find the corresponding read queue. In line 15, the `putnext`(D3DK) function is used to send the message upstream, returning 1 if successful.

```
1   send_error(q,err)
2           queue_t *q;
3           unsigned char err;
4   {
5           mblk_t *bp;
6
7           if ((bp = allocb(1, BPRI_HI)) == NULL) /* allocate msg. block */
8                   return(0);
9
10          bp->b_datap->db_type = M_ERROR;    /* set msg type to M_ERROR */
11          *bp->b_wptr++ = err;               /* increment write pointer */
12
13          if(!q->q_flag & QREADR))           /* if not read queue      */
14                  q = RD(q);                 /*    get read queue      */
15          putnext(q,bp);                     /* send message upstream  */
16          return(1);
17  }
```

backq (D3DK)

NAME
backq – get pointer to the queue behind the current queue

SYNOPSIS
    #include <sys/stream.h>

    queue_t *backq(queue_t *cq);

ARGUMENT
cq The pointer to the current queue. `queue_t` is an alias for the queue(D4DK) structure.

DESCRIPTION
backq returns a pointer to the queue preceding *cq* (the current queue). If *cq* is a read queue, backq returns a pointer to the queue downstream from *cq*, unless it is the stream end. If *cq* is a write queue, backq returns a pointer to the next queue upstream from *cq*, unless it is the stream head.

RETURN VALUE
If successful, backq returns a pointer to the queue preceding the current queue. Otherwise, it returns NULL.

LEVEL
Base or Interrupt

SEE ALSO
BCI Driver Development Guide, Chapter 7, "STREAMS"

bcanput (D3DK)

NAME
bcanput – test for flow control in specified priority band

SYNOPSIS
#include <sys/stream.h>

int bcanput(queue_t *q, unsigned char pri);

ARGUMENT
q   Pointer to the message queue.

pri   Message priority.

DESCRIPTION
Like the canput(D3DK) function, bcanput searches through the stream (starting at *q*) until it finds a queue containing a service routine where the message can be enqueued, or until it reaches the end of the stream. If found, the queue containing the service routine is tested to see if there is room for a message in the queue. If the queue is full, bcanput sets the QWANTW flag to back-enable the caller's service routine.

If *pri* is 0, the bcanput call is equivalent to a call to canput.

NOTE: You are responsible for both testing a queue with bcanput and refraining from placing a message on the queue if bcanput fails.

RETURN VALUE
A 1 is returned if a message of priority *pri* can be placed on the queue, or if the band does not yet exist on the queue. A 0 is returned if the priority band is flow-controlled.

LEVEL
Base or Interrupt

SEE ALSO
BCI Driver Development Guide, Chapter 7, "STREAMS"

canput(D3DK), putbq(D3DK), putnext(D3DK)

bcopy (D3DK)

NAME
bcopy – copy data between address locations in the kernel

SYNOPSIS
`#include <sys/types.h>`

int bcopy(caddr_t *from,* caddr_t *to,* long *bcount*);

ARGUMENTS
from   Source address from which the copy is made.

to   Destination address to which copy is made.

bcount The number of bytes moved.

DESCRIPTION
bcopy copies *bcount* bytes from one kernel address to another. If the input and output addresses overlap, the command executes, but the results may not be as expected.

CAUTION: The *from* and *to* addresses must be within the kernel space. No range checking is done. If an address outside of the kernel space is selected, the driver may corrupt the system in an unpredictable way.

Note that bcopy should never be used to move data in or out of a user buffer, because it has no provision for handling page faults. The user address space can be swapped out at any time, and bcopy always assumes that there will be no paging faults. If bcopy attempts to access the user buffer when it is swapped out, the system will panic. It is safe to use bcopy to move data within kernel space, since kernel space is never swapped out.

RETURN VALUE
Under all conditions, 0 is returned.

LEVEL
Base or Interrupt

SEE ALSO
BCI Driver Development Guide, Chapter 6, "Input/Output Operations"

copyin(D3DK), copyout(D3DK)

EXAMPLE
An I/O request is made for data stored in a RAM disk. If the I/O operation is a read request, the data is copied from the RAM disk to a buffer (line 7). If it is a write request, the data is copied from a buffer to the RAM disk (line 11). The bcopy function is used since both the RAM disk and the buffer are part of the kernel address space.

```
1   #define RAMDNBLK    1000            /* blocks in the RAM disk      */
2   #define RAMDBSIZ    512             /* bytes per block             */
3   char ramdblks[RAMDNBLK][RAMDBSIZ];  /* blocks forming RAM disk    */
        ...
4
5   if (bp->b_flags & B_READ) /* if read request, copy data from RAM  */
6                             /* disk data block to system buffer     */
7       bcopy(&ramdblks[bp->b_blkno][0], bp->b_un.b_addr, bp->b_bcount);
8
```

bcopy(D3DK)   bcopy(D3DK)

```
 9      else                    /* else write request, copy data from a */
10                              /* system buffer to RAM disk data block */
11          bcopy(bp->b_un.b_addr, &ramdblks[bp->b_blkno][0], bp->b_bcount);
```

biodone (D3DK)

NAME
biodone – release buffer after block I/O and wakeup processes

SYNOPSIS
```
#include <sys/types.h>
#include <sys/buf.h>

void biodone(struct buf *bp);
```

ARGUMENT

bp Pointer to the buffer header structure defined in buf.h. This is the address of the buffer header associated with the buffer where the I/O occurred.

DESCRIPTION

The biodone function is called by either the driver int(D2D) or strategy(D2DK) routines when a block I/O request is complete. In general, biodone awakens sleeping processes waiting for the I/O to complete, sets the B_DONE flag in the buf structure b_flags field, and releases the block if the I/O is asynchronous.

For drivers that wish to make multiple I/O requests without releasing and reallocating a buffer header for each individual request, biodone provides the capability to check for an additional function to be called before the buffer header is released. Additional routines to be called from biodone are referenced by the (*b_biodone) field of the buf structure.

biodone performs the following functions in the order presented:

checks the (*biodone) field of the buf structure for additional routines to be called. If an additional routine is referenced, it is called and the functions listed below are not completed.

awakens the process(es) that called sleep(D3DK) to wait for the buffer header if I/O is synchronous

releases the block if I/O is asynchronous and awakens processes awaiting asynchronous I/O

marks b_flags of buffer with B_DONE

RETURN VALUE
None

LEVEL
Base or Interrupt

SEE ALSO

BCI Driver Development Guide, Chapter 9, "Synchronizing Hardware and Software Events"

biowait(D3DK), buf(D4DK), delay(D3DK), int(D3D), strategy(D3DK), sleep(D3DK), timeout(D3DK), untimeout(D3DK), wakeup(D3DK)

EXAMPLE

Generally, the first validation test performed by any block device strategy(D2DK) routine is a check for an end-of-file (EOF) condition. The strategy routine is responsible for determining an EOF condition when the device is accessed directly. If a **read** request is made for one block beyond the limits of the device (line 10), it will report an EOF condition. Otherwise, if the request is outside the limits of the device, the routine will report an error condition. In either case, report the I/O operation as complete (line 27).

```
1    #define RAMDNBLK    1000           /* Number of blocks in RAM disk */
2    #define RAMDBSIZ    512            /* Number of bytes per block */
3    char ramdblks[RAMDNBLK][RAMDBSIZ]; /* Array containing RAM disk */
4
5    ramdstrategy(bp)
6          register struct buf *bp;
7    {
8          register daddr_t blkno = bp->b_blkno;   /* get block number */
9
10         if (blkno < 0 || blkno >= RAMDNBLK) {
11             /*
12              * If requested block is outside RAM disk
13              * limits, test for EOF which could result
14              * from a direct (physiock) request.
15              */
16             if (blkno == RAMDNBLK && bp->b_flags & B_READ) {
17                 /*
18                  * If read is for block beyond RAM disk
19                  * limits, mark EOF condition.
20                  */
21                 bp->b_resid -= bp->b_bcount;/* compute return value */
22
23             } else {                  /* I/O attempt is beyond */
24                 bp->b_error = ENXIO;  /*    limits of RAM disk */
25                 bp->b_flags |= B_ERROR;  /* return error */
26             } /* endif */
27             biodone(bp);              /* mark I/O complete (B_DONE) */
28             /*
29              * Wake any processes awaiting this I/O
30              * or release buffer for asynchronous
31              * (B_ASYNC) request.
32              */
33             return;
34         } /* endif */
       ...
```

biowait(D3DK)   **biowait(D3DK)**

NAME

biowait – suspend processes pending completion of block I/O

SYNOPSIS

```
#include <sys/types.h>
#include <sys/buf.h>

int biowait(struct buf *bp);
```

ARGUMENT

bp   Pointer to the `buf` structure.

DESCRIPTION

The `biowait` function suspends process execution during a block I/O transfer by calling `sleep(D3DK)`. Block driver routines using the `buf` structure to allocate buffers can use the `biowait` function to suspend a process while waiting for a read or write request to complete.

The `biowait` function is one of three functions used to aid block I/O transfers. The other functions in this group are `biodone(D3DK)`, which notifies `biowait` that the I/O is complete, and `brelse`, which frees the buffer allocated for the transfer.

Drivers using the `biowait` function must also include the `biodone(D3DK)` function in their interrupt routines. The `biodone` function awakens `biowait` when the I/O transfer is complete.

Because `biowait` calls `sleep`, `biowait` cannot be called from an interrupt routine or from an `init(D2D)` routine.

RETURN VALUE

None. However, `biowait` returns any error that may have occured during the I/O transfer to the user using `geterror(D3DK)`.

LEVEL

Base Only (Do not call from an interrupt routine)

SEE ALSO

biodone(D3DK), brelse(D3DK), sleep(D3DK), timeout(D3DK), untimeout(D3DK), wakeup(D3DK)

bp_mapin (D3DK)   **bp_mapin (D3DK)**

NAME
bp_mapin – allocate virtual address space

SYNOPSIS
```
#include <sys/types.h>
#include <sys/buf.h>
```
vaddr_t bp_mapin(struct buf *bp);

ARGUMENTS
bp   Pointer to the buffer header structure.

DESCRIPTION
The bp_mapin function is used to map virtual address space to a page list maintaned by the buffer header during a paged-I/O request. bp_mapin allocates system virtual address space, maps that space to the page list, and returns the offset into the map. The offset is stored in the bp->b_un.b_addr field of the of the buf structure (see buf(D4DK)). Virtual address space is then deallocated using the bp_mapout function.

If a NULL page list is encountered, bp_mapin returns without allocating space and no mapping is performed.

RETURN VALUE
The starting address of the allocated system virtual address space.

LEVEL
Base

SEE ALSO
bp_mapout(D3DK), buf(D4DK)

bp_mapout(D3DK)

NAME
bp_mapout – deallocate virtual address space

SYNOPSIS
    #include <sys/types.h>
    #include <sys/buf.h>

    void bp_mapin(struct buf *bp);

ARGUMENTS
bp   Pointer to the buffer header structure.

DESCRIPTION
This function deallocates system virtual address space allocated by a previous call to bp_mapin(D3DK). bp_mapin maps virtual address space to a page list maintained by the buffer header for a paged-I/O request, then returns the offset into the map to the b_addr field of the buf structure.

RETURN VALUE
None

LEVEL
Base

SEE ALSO
bp_mapin(D3DK), buf(D4DK)

btopr (D3DK)   **btopr (D3DK)**

NAME
   btopr – convert size in bytes to size in pages (round up)

SYNOPSIS
   #include <sys/ddi.h>

   unsigned long btopr(unsigned long *numbytes*);

ARGUMENT
   numbytes   Number of bytes.

DESCRIPTION
   This function returns the number of memory pages contained in the specified number of bytes memory, rounded up to the next whole page. For example, if the page size is 2048, then btopr(4096) returns 2, and btopr(4097) returns 3.

RETURN VALUE
   The return value is always the number of pages. There are no invalid input values, and therefore no error return values.

LEVEL
   Base or Interrupt

SEE ALSO
   btop(D3DK), ptob(D3DK)

NAME

bufcall – call a function when a buffer becomes available

SYNOPSIS

```
#include <sys/stream.h>
```

int bufcall(int *size*, int *pri*, int (*func)(), long *arg*);

ARGUMENTS

size   Number of bytes in the buffer.

pri   Priority of the allocb(D3DK) allocation request (not used).

func   Function or driver routine to be called when a buffer becomes available.

arg   Argument to the function to be called when a buffer becomes available.

DESCRIPTION

bufcall serves as a timeout(D3DK) call of indeterminate length. When a buffer allocation request fails, bufcall can be used to schedule the routine *func*, to be called with the argument *arg* when a buffer becomes available. *func* may be a routine that calls bufcall or it may be another kernel function.

NOTE: Even when *func* is called by bufcall, allocb(D3DK) can still fail if another module or driver had allocated the memory before *func* was able to call allocb.

RETURN VALUE

If the bufcall scheduling fails, *func* is never called and 0 is returned. If successful, bufcall returns 1.

LEVEL

Base or Interrupt

SEE ALSO

BCI Driver Development Guide, Chapter 7, "STREAMS"

allocb(D3DK), esballoc(D3DK), esbbcall(D3DK), testb(D3DK), timeout(D3DK)

EXAMPLE

The purpose of this srv(D2DK) service routine is to add a header to all M_DATA messages. Service routines must process all messages on their queues before returning, or arrange to be rescheduled.

While there are message to be processed (line 13), check to see if it is a high priority message or a normal priority message that can be sent on (line 14). Normal priority message that cannot be sent are put back on the message queue (line 34). If the message was a high priority one, or if was normal priority and canput(D3DK) succeeded, then send all but M_DATA messages to the next stream entity with putnext(D3DK) (line16).

For M_DATA messages, try to allocate a buffer large enough to hold the header (line 18). If no such buffer is available, the service routine must be rescheduled for a time when a buffer is available. The original message is put back on the queue (line 20) and bufcall (line 21) is used to attempt the rescheduling. It

bufcall(D3DK)

will succeed if a buffer of the specified size (`sizeof (struct hdr)`) is available. If it does, `qenable`(D3DK) will put q on the list of queues to have their service routines called. If `bufcall` fails, `timeout`(D3DK) (line 22) is used to try again in about a half second (`HZ/2`).

If the buffer allocation was successful, initialize the header (lines 25–28), make the message type `M_PROTO` (line 29), link the `M_DATA` message to it (line 30), and pass it on (line 31).

```
1   struct hdr {
2          unsigned int h_size;
3          int          h_version;
4   };
5
6   modsrv(q)
7          queue_t *q;
8   {
9          mblk_t *bp;
10         mblk_t *mp;
11         struct hdr *hp;
12
13         while ((mp = getq(q)) != NULL) {          /* get next message */
14            if (mp->b_datap->db_type >= QPCTL ||   /* if high priority */
                  canput(q->q_next)) {               /* normal & can be passed */
15               if (mp->b_datap->db_type != M_DATA)
16                  putnext(q, mp);                  /* send all but M_DATA */
17               else {
18                  bp = allocb(sizeof(struct hdr), BPRI_LO);
19                  if (bp == NULL) {                /* if unsuccessful */
20                     putbq(q, mp);                 /* put it back */
21                     if (!bufcall(sizeof(struct hdr), BPRI_LO,
                             qenable, (long)q))     /* try to reschedule */
22                        timeout(qenable, (long)q, HZ/2);
23                     return;
24                  }
25                  hp = (struct hdr *)bp->b_wptr;
26                  hp->h_size = msgdsize(mp);       /* initialize header */
27                  hp->h_version = 1;
28                  bp->b_wptr += sizeof(struct hdr);
29                  bp->b_datap->db_type = M_PROTO;  /* make M_PROTO  */
30                  bp->b_cont = mp;                 /* link it */
31                  putnext(q, bp);                  /* pass it on */
32               }
33            } else {                               /* normal priority, canput failed */
34               putbq(q, mp);                       /* put back on the message queue */
35               return;
36            }
37         }
38  }
```

bzero (D3DK)　　　　　　　　　　　　　　　　　　　　　　　　　　**bzero (D3DK)**

NAME
bzero – clear memory for a given number of bytes

SYNOPSIS
```
#include <sys/types.h>

int bzero(caddr_t addr, int bytes);
```

ARGUMENTS
addr　　Starting virtual address of memory to be cleared.

bytes　　The number of bytes to clear starting at *addr*.

DESCRIPTION
The `bzero` function clears a contiguous portion of memory by filling the memory with zeros.

CAUTION: The address range specified must be within the kernel space. No range checking is done. If an address outside of the kernel space is selected, the driver may corrupt the system in an unpredictable way.

RETURN VALUE
Under normal conditions, a `0` is returned. Otherwise, a `-1` is returned.

LEVEL
Base or Interrupt

SEE ALSO
`bcopy`(D3DK), `clrbuf`(D3DK), `kmem_zalloc`(D3DK)

EXAMPLE
In a driver `close`(D2DK) routine, rather than clear each individual member of its private data structure, the driver could use `bzero` as shown here:

```
bzero(&drv_dat[minor(dev)], sizeof(struct drvr_data));
```

canput (D3DK)

NAME
canput – test for room in a message queue

SYNOPSIS
```
#include <sys/stream.h>

int canput(queue_t *cq);
```

ARGUMENT
cq The pointer to the message queue. queue_t is an alias for the queue(D4DK) structure.

DESCRIPTION
canput searches through the stream (starting at *cq*) until it finds a queue containing a service routine where the message can be enqueued, or until it reaches the end of the stream. If found, the queue containing the service routine is tested to see if there is room for a message in the queue. If the queue is full, canput sets the QWANTW flag to back-enable the caller's service routine.

NOTE: You are responsible for both testing a queue with canput and refraining from placing a message on the queue if canput fails.

RETURN VALUE
If the message queue is not full, 1 is returned. A 0 is returned if the queue is full.

LEVEL
Base or Interrupt

SEE ALSO
BCI Driver Development Guide, Chapter 7, "STREAMS"

bcanput(D3DK), putbq(D3DK), putnext(D3DK)

EXAMPLE
See the bufcall(D3DK) function page for an example of canput.

clrbuf(D3DK)   **clrbuf(D3DK)**

NAME
clrbuf – erase the contents of a buffer

SYNOPSIS
```
#include <sys/types.h>
#include <sys/buf.h>

void clrbuf(struct buf *bp);
```

ARGUMENT
bp   Pointer to the buf(D4DK) structure

DESCRIPTION
The `clrbuf` function zeros a buffer and sets the `b_resid` member of the buf structure to 0. Zeros are placed in the buffer starting at `bp->b_un.b_words` for a length of `bp->b_bcount` bytes. `b_un.b_words` and `b_bcount` are members of the buf structure defined in `sys/buf.h`.

RETURN VALUE
None

LEVEL
Base or Interrupt

SEE ALSO
brelse(D3DK), buf(D4DK)

EXAMPLE
See `biowait`(D3DK).

cmn_err (D3DK)

NAME

cmn_err – display an error message or panic the system

SYNOPSIS

```
#include <sys/cmn_err.h>

int cmn_err( int level, char *format, int args);
```

ARGUMENTS

level A constant defined in the `sys/cmn_err.h` header file. *level* indicates the severity of the error condition. The four severity levels are

- CE_CONT — used to continue another message or to display an informative message not connected with an error.

- CE_NOTE — used to display a message preceded with NOTICE. This message is used to report system events that do not necessarily require user action, but may interest the system administrator. For example, a message saying that a sector on a disk needs to be accessed repeatedly before it can be accessed correctly might be noteworthy.

- CE_WARN — used to display a message preceded with WARNING. This message is used to report system events that require immediate attention, such as those where if an action is not taken, the system may panic. For example, when a peripheral device does not initialize correctly, this level should be used.

- CE_PANIC — used to display a message preceded with PANIC or DOUBLE PANIC, and to panic the system. Drivers should specify this level only under the most severe conditions or when debugging a driver. A valid use of this level is when the system cannot continue to function. If the error is recoverable, or not essential to continued system operation, do not panic the system. This level halts multiuser processing.

format The message to be displayed. By default, the message is sent both to the system console and to the kernel buffer `putbuf`. If the first character in *format* is an exclamation point ("!"), the message goes only to putbuf. If the first character in *format* is a circumflex ("^"), the message goes only to the console. Except for the first character, the rules for *format* are the same as those for `printf`(3S) strings. To read putbuf, use the following `crash`(1M) commands:

```
od -d putbufsz
od -a putbuf size
```

The first command returns the size of `putbuf` (the default is 2000 bytes). The second command uses the returned *size* to read `putbuf`.

cmn_err (D3DK) cmn_err (D3DK)

cmn_err appends \n to each *format*, even when a message is sent to putbuf, except when *level* is CE_CONT.

Vaild conversion specifications are %s, %u, %d, %o, and %x. The cmn_err function is otherwise similar to the printf(3S) library subroutine in displaying messages on the system console or storing on putbuf.

NOTE: cmn_err does not accept length specifications in conversion specifications. For example, %3d is ignored.

args the set of arguments passed with the message being displayed. Any argument within the range of supported conversion specifications can be passed.

DESCRIPTION

cmn_err displays a specified message on the console and/or stores it in the putbuf array. cmn_err can also panic the system.

At times, a driver may encounter error conditions requiring the attention of a primary or secondary system console monitor. These conditions may mean halting multiuser processing; however, this must be done with caution. Except during the debugging stage, a driver should never stop the system.

The cmn_err function with the CE_CONT argument can be used by driver developers as a driver code debugging tool. However, using cmn_err in this capacity can change system timing characteristics.

If CE_PANIC is set, cmn_err stops the machine.

RETURN VALUE

None. However, if an unknown *level* is passed to cmn_err, the following panic error message is displayed:

PANIC: unknown level in cmn_err (level=*level*, msg=*format*)

LEVEL

Base or Interrupt

SEE ALSO

BCI Driver Development Guide, Chapter 12

print(D2DK), printf(3S)

EXAMPLE

The cmn_err function can record tracing and debugging information only in the putbuf (lines 15 and 16); display problems with a device only on the system console (line 21); or stop the system if a required device malfunctions (line 27).

```
1    struct  device {           /* physical device registers layout */
2            int     control;   /* physical device control word */
3            int     status;    /* physical device status word */
4            int     error;     /* error codes from device */
5            short   recv_char; /* receive character from device */
6            short   xmit_char; /* transmit character to device */
7    }; /* end device */
8
9    extern struct device xx_addr[];     /* physical device registers */
10   extern int           xx_cnt;        /* number of physical devices */
```

```
  11     register struct device *rp;
  12     rp = xx_addr[(getminor(dev) >> 4) & 0xf];        /* get dev registers */
  13
  14     #ifdef DEBUG                     /* in debugging mode, log function call */
  15         cmn_err(CE_NOTE, "!xx_open function call, dev = 0x%x", dev);
  16         cmn_err(CE_CONT, "! flag = 0x%x", flag);      /* continue msg */
  17     #endif  /* end DEBUG */
  18
  19                         /* display device power failure on system console */
  20         if ((rp->status & POWER) == OFF)
  21             cmn_err(CE_WARN, "xx_open: Power is OFF on device %d port %d",
  22                     ((getminor(dev) >> 4) & 0xf), (getminor(dev) & 0xf));
  23
  24                         /* halt system if root device has bad VTOC */
  25                         /* send message to system console and to putbuf */
  26         if (rp->error == BADVTOC && dev == rootdev)
  27             cmn_err(CE_PANIC, "xx_open: Bad VTOC on root device");
```

copyb (D3DK)   **copyb (D3DK)**

NAME
copyb – copy a message block

SYNOPSIS
```
#include <sys/stream.h>

mblk_t *copyb(mblk_t *bp);
```

ARGUMENT
bp   Pointer to the message block from which data is copied.

DESCRIPTION
copyb allocates a new message block, and copies into it the data from the block pointed to by *bp*. The new block will be at least as large as the block being copied. The b_rptr and b_wptr members of *bp* are used to determine how many bytes to copy.

RETURN VALUE
If successful, copyb returns a pointer to the newly allocated message block containing the copied data. Otherwise, it returns a NULL pointer.

LEVEL
Base or Interrupt

SEE ALSO
BCI Driver Development Guide, Chapter 7, "STREAMS"

allocb(D3DK)

EXAMPLE
For each message in the list, test to see if the downstream queue is full with the canput(D3DK) function (line 21). If it is not full, use copyb(D3DK) to copy a header message block, and dupmsg(D3DK) to duplicate the data to be retransmitted. If either operation fails, reschedule a timeout at the next valid interval.

Update the new header block with the correct destination address (line 34), link the message to it (line 35), and send it downstream (line 36). At the end of the list, reschedule this routine.

```
1    struct retrns {
2          mblk_t *r_mp;
3          long r_address;
4          queue_t *r_outq;
5          struct retrns *r_next;
6    };
7
8    struct protoheader {
           . . .
9          long h_address;
           . . .
10   };
11
12   mblk_t *header;
13
14   retransmit(ret)
```

copyb (D3DK)

```
15              register struct retrns *ret;
16      {
17              register mblk_t *bp, *mp;
18              struct protoheader *php;
19
20              while (ret) {
21                      if (!canput(ret->r_outq->q_next)) { /* no room */
22                              ret = ret->r_next;
23                              continue;
24                      }
25                      bp = copyb(header);    /* copy header msg. block */
26                      if (bp == NULL)
27                              break;
28                      mp = dupmsg(ret->r_mp);      /* duplicate data */
29                      if (mp == NULL) {            /* if unsuccessful */
30                              freeb(bp);           /* free the block */
31                              break;
32                      }
33                      php = (struct protoheader *)bp->b_rptr;
34                      php->h_address = ret->r_address; /* new header */
35                      bp->bp_cont = mp;            /* link the message */
36                      putnext(ret->r_outq, bp);    /* send downstream */
37                      ret = ret->r_next;
38              }
39              timeout(retransmit, (long)ret, RETRNS_TIME);  /* reschedule */
40      }
```

copyin (D3DK)

NAME
copyin – copy data from a user program to a driver buffer

SYNOPSIS
```
#include <sys/types.h>
```
int copyin(caddr_t *userbuf,* caddr_t *driverbuf,* int *cn*);

ARGUMENTS
userbuf   User program source address from which data is transferred.

driverbuf   Driver destination address to which data is transferred.

cn   Number of bytes transferred.

DESCRIPTION
copyin copies data from a user program source address to a driver buffer. The driver developer must ensure that adequate space is allocated for the destination address.

Addresses that are word-aligned are moved most efficiently. However, the driver developer is not obligated to ensure alignment. This function automatically finds the most efficient move according to address alignment.

RETURN VALUE
Under normal conditions a 0 is returned indicating a successful copy. A −1 is returned if one of the following occurs:

> paging fault; the driver tried to access a page of memory for which it did not have read or write access

> invalid user area or stack area

> invalid address that would have resulted in data being copied into the user block

If a −1 is returned, return `EFAULT`.

LEVEL
Base Only (Do not call from an interrupt routine)

SEE ALSO
BCI Driver Development Guide, Chapter 6, "Input/Output Operations"

bcopy(D3DK), copyout(D3DK), uiomove(D3DK)

copymsg (D3DK)   copymsg (D3DK)

NAME
copymsg – copy a message

SYNOPSIS
#include <sys/stream.h>

mblk_t *copymsg(mblk_t *mp);

ARGUMENTS
mp   Pointer to the message to be copied. mblk_t is an instance of the msgb(D4DK) structure.

DESCRIPTION
copymsg forms a new message by allocating new message blocks, copies the contents of the message referred to by *mp* (using the copyb(D3DK) function), and returns a pointer to the new message.

RETURN VALUE
If the copy is successful, copymsg returns a pointer to the new message. Otherwise, it returns a NULL pointer.

LEVEL
Base or Interrupt

SEE ALSO
BCI Driver Development Guide, Chapter 7, "STREAMS"

allocb(D3DK), copyb(D3DK), msgb(D4DK)

EXAMPLE
The routine lctouc converts all the lowercase ASCII characters in the message to uppercase. If the reference count is greater than one (line 8), then the message is shared, and must be copied before changing the contents of the data buffer. If the call to the copymsg(D3DK) function fails (line 9), return NULL (line 10), otherwise, free the original message (line 11). If the reference count was equal to 1, the message can be modified. For each character (line 16) in each message block (line 15), if it is a lowercase letter, convert it to an uppercase letter line 18). A pointer to the converted message is returned (line 21).

```
1    mblk_t *lctouc(mp)
2       mblk_t *mp;
3    {
4       mblk_t *cmp;
5       mblk_t *tmp;
6       unsigned char *cp;
7
8       if (mp->b_datap->db_ref > 1) {
9           if ((cmp = copymsg(mp)) == NULL)
10              return(NULL);
11          freemsg(mp);
12      } else {
13          cmp = mp;
14      }
15      for (tmp = cmp; tmp; tmp = tmp->b_next) {
16          for (cp = tmp->b_rptr; cp < tmp->b_wptr; cp++) {
```

```
17                  if ((*cp <= 'z') && (*cp >= 'a'))
18                          *cp -= 0x20;
19          }
20      }
21      return(cmp);
22  }
```

copyout (D3DK)

NAME
copyout – copy data from a driver to a user program

SYNOPSIS
```
#include <sys/types.h>
```
int copyout(caddr_t *driverbuf*, caddr_t *userbuf*, long *cn*);

ARGUMENTS
driverbuf Source address in the driver from which the data is transferred.

userbuf Destination address in the user program to which the data is transferred.

cn Number of bytes moved.

DESCRIPTION
copyout copies data from driver buffers to user data space.

Addresses that are word-aligned are moved most efficiently. However, the driver developer is not obligated to ensure alignment. This function automatically finds the most efficient move algorithm according to address alignment.

RETURN VALUE
Under normal conditions a 0 is returned to indicate a successful copy. Otherwise, a –1 is returned if the specified address range is not valid.

If a –1 is returned, return EFAULT.

LEVEL
Base Only (Do not call from an interrupt routine)

SEE ALSO
BCI Driver Development Guide, Chapter 6, "Input/Output Operations"

bcopy(D3DK), uiomove(D3DK), copyin(D3DK)

EXAMPLE
A driver ioctl(D2DK) routine (line 9) can be used to get or set device attributes or registers. In the XX_GETREGS condition (line 17), the driver copies the current device register values to a user data area (line 18). If the specified argument contains an invalid address, an error code is returned.

```
1    struct device {      /* layout of physical device registers */
2           int      control;    /* physical device control word */
3           int      status;     /* physical device status word */
4           short    recv_char;  /* receive character from device */
5           short    xmit_char;  /* transmit character to device */
6    }; /* end device */
7
8    extern struct device xx_addr[]; /* phys. device regs. location */
         . . .
9    xx_ioctl(dev, cmd, arg, flag)
10          dev_t    dev;
11          caddr_t arg;
12                   ...
13   {
14          register struct device *rp = &xx_addr[getminor(dev) >> 4];
```

```
15      switch(cmd)   {
16
17        case XX_GETREGS:     /* copy device regs. to user program */
18            if (copyout((caddr_t)rp, arg, sizeof(struct device))
19                return(EFAULT);
20                /* endif */
21            break;
```

datamsg (D3DK) datamsg (D3DK)

NAME
datamsg – test whether a message is a data message

SYNOPSIS
```
#include <sys/stream.h>
#include <sys/ddi.h>

int datamsg(unsigned char type);
```

ARGUMENT
type   The type of message to be tested. The `db_type` field of the `datab` structure contains the message type. This field may be accessed through the message block using `mp->b_datap->db_type`.

DESCRIPTION
The `datamsg` function tests the type of message to determine if it is a data message type (M_DATA, M_DELAY, M_PROTO, or M_PCPROTO).

RETURN VALUE
`datamsg` returns 1 for TRUE, if the message is a data message; and 0 for FALSE for any other type of message.

LEVEL
Base or Interrupt

SEE ALSO
BCI Driver Development Guide, Chapter 7, "STREAMS"

`allocb`(D3DK), `datab`(D4DK), `msgb`(D4DK)

EXAMPLE
The `put`(D2DK) routine enqueues all data messages for handling by the `srv`(D2DK) (service) routine. All non-data messages are handled in the put routine.

```
 1   xxxput(q, mp)
 2        queue_t *q;
 3        mblk_t *mp;
 4   {
 5     if (datamsg(mp->b_datap->db_type)) {
 6          putq(q, mp);
 7          return;
 8     }
 9     switch (mp->b_datap->db_type) {
10         case M_FLUSH:
              . . .
11     }
12   }
```

delay (D3DK)   **delay (D3DK)**

NAME

delay – delay process execution for a specified number of clock ticks

SYNOPSIS

void delay(long *ticks*);

ARGUMENT

ticks   The number of clock cycles for a delay. *ticks* are frequently set as an expression containing the system variable HZ, the number of clock ticks in one second; HZ is defined in sys/param.h.

DESCRIPTION

delay provides a way to wait for an event to happen. Occasionally, a driver may need to wait a given period of time until work is available. The value of HZ can vary from system to system, and so the function drv_hztousec(D3DK) should be used when accurate timing is required.

The delay function calls timeout(D3DK) to schedule a wakeup call after the specified amount of time has elapsed. delay then goes to sleep until timeout wakes up the sleeping process. While delay is active, splhi is set. At completion, the former priority level is returned through splx.

delay requires user context.

RETURN VALUE

None

LEVEL

Base Only (Do not call from an interrupt routine)

SEE ALSO

BCI Driver Development Guide, Chapter 10, "Synchronizing Hardware and Software Events"

biodone(D3DK), biowait(D3DK), drv_hztousec(D3DK),
drv_usectohz(D3DK), sleep(D3DK), timeout(D3DK), untimeout(D3DK),
wakeup(D3DK)

EXAMPLE

Before a driver I/O routine allocates buffers and stores any user data in them, it checks the status of the device (line 12). If the device needs manual intervention (such as, needing to be refilled with paper), a message is displayed on the system console (line 14). The driver waits an allotted time (line 16) before repeating the procedure.

```
1   struct  device  {           /* layout of physical device registers */
2           int     control;    /* physical device control word       */
3           int     status;     /* physical device status word        */
4           short   xmit_char;  /* transmit character to device       */
5   }; /* end device */
6
7   extern struct device xx_addr[]; /* physical device regs. location */
        . . .
9                                           /* get device registers   */
10  register struct device *rp = &xx_addr[getminor(dev)>>4)];
11
```

delay (D3DK)   **delay (D3DK)**

```
12    while(rp->status & NOPAPER) {      /* while printer is out of paper */
13                        /* display message and ring bell on system console */
14        cmn_err(CE_WARN, "^xx_write: NO PAPER in printer %d\007",
15                    (dev & 0xf));
16        delay(60 * HZ);              /* wait one minute and try again */
17    } /* endwhile */
```

dma_pageio(D3D) **dma_pageio(D3D)**

NAME
dma_pageio – break up an I/O request into manageable units

SYNOPSIS
#include <sys/buf.h>

void dma_pageio(void (*strat)() *strat,* struct buf *bp);

ARGUMENTS
strat   Pointer to the **strategy**(D2DK) routine to call to complete the I/O transfer.

bp   Pointer to the **buf** structure.

DESCRIPTION
dma_pageio breaks up a data transfer request from **physiock**(D3DK) into units of contiguous memory. This function enhances the capabilities of the direct memory access controller (DMAC). The data is broken into 512-byte sectors until the last data bytes are encountered. **dma_pageio** executes **spl0** around its internal **sleep** calls on reads and writes after the **strategy** routine is called. This may alter previously set **spl**(D3D) calls.

The driver must modify **b_flags** to indicate whether the transfer is a read or a write. OR in **B_READ** to indicate a read; turn **B_READ** off to indicate a write.

RETURN VALUE
None. However, conditions in **dma_pageio** can cause the following to be set:

If memory for a temporary buffer cannot be allocated, **b_flags** is ORed with **B_ERROR** and **B_DONE**, and **b_error** is set to **EAGAIN** (resource temporarily unavailable). All allocated temporary buffers are deallocated when the transfer completes.

If the I/O transfer is incomplete (**b_flags** does not contain **B_DONE**), then **b_flags** is set to **B_WANTED** and **sleep**(D3DK) is called to wait until a buffer can be allocated. The **sleep** priority is set to **PRIBIO**.

The **sleep** code section is surrounded by a **spl6-spl0** function set which may alter a previously set **spl** value.

If **B_ERROR** is set after the **strategy**(D2DK) routine completes, allocated memory is freed and **dma_pageio** returns.

When the transfer completes, any allocated buffers are freed.

LEVEL
Base Only

SEE ALSO
BCI Driver Development Guide, Chapter 6, "Input/Output Operations"

EXAMPLE
The following example shows how **dma_pageio** is used when reading or writing disk data.

```
1   struct  dsize   {
2           daddr_t nblocks;  /* number of blocks in disk partition   */
3           int     cyloff;   /* starting cylinder # of partition     */
4   } my_sizes[4] = {
```

dma_pageio (D3D)

```
5
6               20448, 21,         /* partition 0 - cyl 21-305        */
7               21888, 1,          /* partition 1 - cyl  1-305        */
8   };
9
10  /*     physical read    */
11  my_read(dev, uio_p, cred_p)
12          dev_t   dev;
13          uio_t   *uio_p;
14          cred_t  *cred_p;
15  {
16          register int nblks;
17          /* get number of blocks in the partition                   */
18          nblks = my_sizes[getminor(dev) & 0x7].nblocks;
19
20          /* if request is within limits for the device, schedule I/O*/
21          physiock(my_breakup, 0, dev, B_READ, nblks, uio_p);
22
23  }
24  /*     physical write   */
25  my_write(dev, uio_p, cred_p)
26          dev_t   dev;
27          uio_t   *uio_p;
28          cred_t  *cred_p;
29  {
30          register int nblks;
31          /* get the number of blocks in the partition               */
32          nblks = my_sizes[getminor(dev) & 0x7].nblocks;
33
34          /* if request is within limits for the device, schedule I/O */
35           physiock(my_breakup, 0, dev, B_WRITE, nblks, uio_p);
36           }
37  }
38  /*
39   *    break up the request that came from physio into chunks of
40   *    contiguous memory.  Pass at least 512 bytes (one sector) at a
41   *    time (except for the last request).
42   */
43
44  static
45  my_breakup(bp)
46          register struct buf *bp;
47  {
48          dma_pageio(my_strategy, bp);
49  }
```

drv_getparm(D3DK) drv_getparm(D3DK)

NAME
drv_getparm – retrieve kernel state information

SYNOPSIS
    #include <sys/ddi.h>

    int drv_getparm(unsigned long *parm*, unsigned long **value_p*);

ARGUMENTS
parm   The kernel parameter to be obtained from ddi.h. Possible values are

- **LBOLT**   Read the value of the lbolt. (lbolt is an integer that represents the number of clock ticks since the last system reboot. This value is used as a counter or timer inside the system kernel.)
- **PPGRP**   Read the process group identification number. This number determines which processes should receive a HANGUP or BREAK signal when detected by a driver.
- **UPROCP**   Read the process table token value. This information is used for the second argument of the vtop(D3D) function.
- **PPID**   Read process identification number.
- **PSID**   Read process session identification number.
- **TIME**   Read time in seconds.

value_p   A pointer to the data space in which the value of the parameter is to be copied.

DESCRIPTION
This function verifies that *parm* corresponds to a kernel parameter that may be read. If the value of *parm* does not correspond to a parameter or corresponds to a parameter that may not be read, −1 is returned. Otherwise, the value of the parameter is stored in the data space pointed to by *value_p*.

drv_getparm does not explicitly check to see whether the device has the appropriate context when the function is called and the function does not check for correct alignment in the data space pointed to by *value_p*. It is the responsibility of the driver writer to use this function only when it is appropriate to do so and to correctly declare the data space needed by the driver.

RETURN VALUE
drv_getparm returns 0 to indicate success, −1 to indicate failure. The value stored in the space pointed to by *value_p* is the value of the parameter if 0 is returned, undefined if −1 is returned. −1 is returned if you specify a value other than LBOLT, PPGRP, PPID, PSID, TIME or UPROCP. Always check the return code when using this function.

LEVEL
Base only when using the PPGRP, PPID, PSID, TIME, or UPROCP argument values.

drv_getparm (D3DK)

Interrupt usable when using the `LBOLT` argument value.

SEE ALSO
  vtop(D3D), buf(D4DK)

drv_hztousec (D3DK)   **drv_hztousec (D3DK)**

NAME
   drv_hztousec – convert clock ticks to microseconds

SYNOPSIS
   ```
   #include <sys/types.h>
   #include <sys/ddi.h>

   clock_t drv_hztousec(clock_t hz);
   ```

ARGUMENT
   hz   The length of time (expressed in HZ units) to convert to its microsecond equivalent

DESCRIPTION
   drv_hztousec converts into microseconds the length of time expressed by *hz*, which is in units of time based on the value of HZ, the kernel parameter whose value is defined in sys/param.h.

   The kernel variable lbolt, which is readable through drv_getparm(D3DK), is the length of time the system has been up since boot and is expressed in HZ units. Drivers often use the value of lbolt before and after an I/O request to measure the amount of time it took the device to process the request. drv_hztousec can be used by the driver to convert the reading from HZ units, which could potentially vary between system implementations, to a known unit of time.

RETURN VALUE
   The number of microseconds equivalent to the *hz* argument. No error value is returned. If the microsecond equivalent to *hz* is too large to be represented as a clock_t, then the maximum clock_t value will be returned.

LEVEL
   Base or Interrupt

SEE ALSO
   drv_getparm(D3DK), drv_usectohz(D3DK)

drv_priv(D3DK)

NAME
drv_priv – determine driver privilege

SYNOPSIS
int drv_priv(cred_t *cr);

ARGUMENT
cr Pointer to the cred(D4DK) (credential) structure.

DESCRIPTION
The drv_priv function provides a general interface to the system privilege policy. It determines whether the credentials supplied by the cred structure pointed to by *cr* identify a priviledged process. This function should only be used when file access modes and special minor device numbers are insufficient to provide protection for the requested driver function. It is intended to replace all calls to suser() and any explicit checks for effective user ID = 0 in driver code.

RETURN VALUE
This routine returns 0 if it succeeds, EPERM if it fails.

LEVEL
Base or Interrupt

SEE ALSO
cred(D4DK)

NAME

drv_usectohz – convert microseconds to clock ticks

SYNOPSIS

```
#include <sys/types.h>
#include <sys/ddi.h>
```

clock_t drv_usectohz(clock_t *microsecs*);

ARGUMENTS

microsecs   The number of microseconds to convert to its HZ equivalent.

DESCRIPTION

drv_usectohz converts a length of time expressed in microseconds to HZ, the unit of time based on the the kernel parameter HZ whose value is defined in sys/param.h. The time arguments to timeout(D3DK) and delay(D3DK) are expressed in HZ, as well as the kernel variable lbolt, which is readable through drv_getparm(LBOLT).

drv_usectohz is a portable way for drivers to make calls to timeout(D3DK) and delay(D3DK) and remain binary compatible should the driver object file be made part of a kernel that was compiled with a value of HZ different from that with which the driver was compiled.

RETURN VALUE

The value returned is the number of HZ units equivalent to the *microsecs* argument. No error value is returned. If the HZ equivalent to *microsecs* is too large to be represented as a clock_t, then the maximum clock_t value will be returned.

LEVEL

Base or Interrupt

SEE ALSO

drv_hztousec(D3DK)

drv_usecwait (D3DK)

NAME
drv_usecwait – busy-wait for specified interval

SYNOPSIS
```
#include <sys/types.h>
#include <sys/ddi.h>

void drv_usecwait(clock_t microsecs);
```

ARGUMENT
microsecs   The number of microseconds to busy-wait.

DESCRIPTION
The kernel function `delay`(D3DK) can be used by a driver to delay for a specified number of system ticks (given by parameter `HZ` in `sys/param.h`, which indicates how many system ticks occur per second). There are two limitations: (1) the granularity of the wait time is limited to `1/HZ` second, which may be more time than is needed for the delay, and (2) `delay`(D3DK) may only be invoked with user context and hence cannot be used at interrupt time or system initialization.

Often, drivers need to delay for only a few microseconds, waiting for a write to a device register to be picked up by the device. In this case, even with user context, `delay`(D3DK) produces too long a wait period. The function `drv_usecwait` is provided to give drivers a means of busy-waiting for a specified microsecond count. The amount of time spent busy-waiting may be greater than the microsecond count but will minimally be the number of microseconds specified.

Note that the driver wastes processor time by making this call since `drv_usecwait` does not invoke sleep but simply busy-waits. The driver should only make calls to `drv_usecwait` as needed, and only for as much time as needed. `drv_usecwait` does not raise the processor interrupt level; if the driver wishes to mask out interrupts, it is its responsibility to set the priority level before the call and restore it to its original value afterward.

RETURN VALUE
None

LEVEL
Base or Interrupt

SEE ALSO
`delay`(D3DK), `timeout`(D3DK), `untimeout`(D3DK)

dupb(D3DK)　　　　　　　　　　　　　　　　　　　　　　　　　　　　　　　　　　**dupb(D3DK)**

NAME
    dupb – duplicate a message block descriptor

SYNOPSIS
    #include <sys/stream.h>

    mblk_t *dupb(mblk_t *bp);

ARGUMENTS
    bp　　　Pointer to the message block to be duplicated. mblk_t is an instance of the msgb(D4DK) structure.

DESCRIPTION
    dupb creates a new mblk_t structure to reference the message block pointed to by *bp*. Unlike copyb(D3DK), dupb does not copy the information in the data block, but creates a new structure to point to it.

    The following figure shows how the db_ref field of the dblk_t structure has been changed from 1 to 2, reflecting the increase in the number of references to the data block. The new mblk_t contains the same information as the first. Note that b_rptr and b_wptr are copied from *bp*, and that db_ref is incremented.

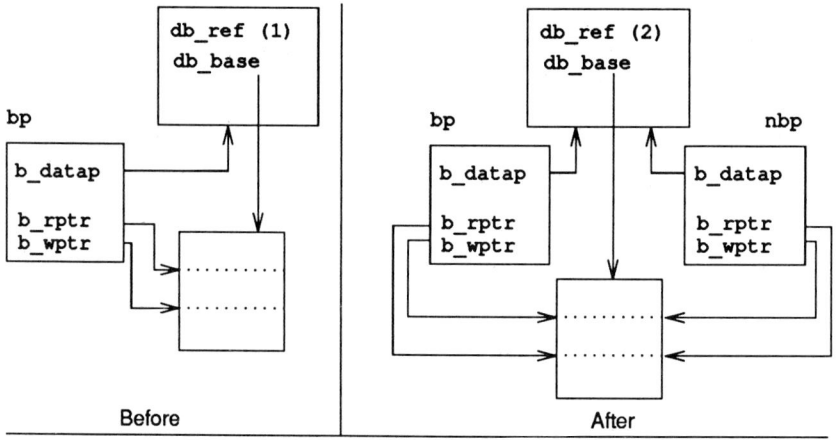

nbp=dupb(bp);

RETURN VALUE
    If successful, dupb returns a pointer to the new message block. Otherwise, it returns a NULL pointer.

LEVEL
    Base or Interrupt

SEE ALSO
    copyb(D3DK)

dupb(D3DK)

EXAMPLE

This `srv`(D3DK) (service) routine adds a header to all `M_DATA` messages before passing them along. The message block for the header was allocated elsewhere. For each message on the queue, if it is a priority message, pass it along immediately (lines 9-10). Otherwise, if it is anything other than an `M_DATA` message (line 11), and if it can be sent along (line 12), then do so (line 13). Otherwise, put the message back on the queue and return (lines 15-16). For all `M_DATA` messages, first check to see if the stream is flow-controlled (line 19). If it is, put the message back on the queue and return (line 22); if it is not, the header block is duplicated (line 20). If dupb fails, the service routine is rescheduled in one tenth of a second (HZ/10) with `timeout` and then we return (lines 23-24). If dupb succeeds, link the `M_DATA` message to it (line 26) and pass it along (line 27). dupb can be used here instead of copyb(D3DK) because the contents of the header block are not changed.

```
1   xxxsrv(q)
2       queue_t *q;
3   {
4       mblk_t *mp;
5       mblk_t *bp;
6       extern mblk_t *hdr;
7
8       while ((mp = getq(q)) != NULL) {
9           if (mp->b_datap->db_type >= QPCTL) {
10              putnext(q, mp);
11          } else if (mp->b_datap->db_type != M_DATA) {
12              if (canput(q->q_next))
13                  putnext(q, mp);
14              else {
15                  putbq(q, mp);
16                  return;
17              }
18          } else {      /* M_DATA */
19              if (canput(q->q_next)) {
20                  bp = dupb(hdr);
21                  if (bp == NULL) {
22                      putbq(q, mp);
23                      timeout(qenable, (long)q, HZ/10);
24                      return;
25                  }
26                  linkb(bp, mp);
27                  putnext(q, bp);
28              } else {
29                  putbq(q, mp);
30                  return;
31              }
32          }
33      }
34  }
```

dupmsg (D3DK)

NAME
dupmsg – duplicate a message

SYNOPSIS
#include <sys/stream.h>

mblk_t *dupmsg(mblk_t *mp);

ARGUMENTS
mp   Pointer to the message block.

DESCRIPTION
dupmsg forms a new message by copying the message block descriptors pointed to by *mp* and linking them. dupb(D3DK) is called for each message block. The data blocks themselves are not duplicated.

RETURN VALUE
If successful, dupmsg returns a pointer to the new message block. Otherwise, it returns a NULL pointer.

LEVEL
Base or Interrupt

SEE ALSO
BCI Driver Development Guide, Chapter 7, "STREAMS"

copyb(D3DK), copymsg(D3DK), dupb(D3DK)

EXAMPLE
See the copyb(D3DK) function page for an example of dupmsg.

enableok(D3DK)   enableok(D3DK)

NAME
enableok – reschedule a queue for service

SYNOPSIS
```
#include <sys/stream.h>
#include <sys/ddi.h>

void enableok(queue_t *q);
```

ARGUMENT
q   A pointer to the queue to be rescheduled.

DESCRIPTION
The **enableok** function allows queue *q* to be rescheduled for service. It cancels the effect of a previous use of the **noenable**(D3DK) function on *q* by turning off the QNOENB flag in the queue.

RETURN VALUE
None

LEVEL
Base or Interrupt

SEE ALSO
BCI Driver Development Guide, Chapter 7, "STREAMS"

noenable(D3DK), qenable(D3DK)

EXAMPLE
The **qrestart** routine uses two STREAMS functions to restart a queue that has been disabled. The **enableok** function turns off the QNOENB flag, allowing the **qenable**(D3DK) function to schedule the queue for immediate processing.

```
 1  void
 2  qrestart(rdwr_q)
 3      register queue_t *rdwr_q;
 4
 5  {
 6      enableok(rdwr_q);
 7      /* re-enable a queue that has been disabled */
 8      (void) qenable(rdwr_q);
 9
10  }
```

esballoc(D3DK)

NAME
esballoc – allocate a message block using a shared buffer

SYNOPSIS
```
#include <sys/stream.h>
```
mblk_t *esballoc(unsigned char *base, int size, int pri,
    frtn_t *fr_rtnp);

ARGUMENTS
- *base* — Address of user supplied data buffer.
- *size* — Number of bytes in data buffer.
- *pri* — Priority of allocation request (to be used by allocb(D3DK) function, called by esballoc).
- *fr_rtnp* — Free routine data structure.

DESCRIPTION
esballoc creates a STREAMS message and attaches a user-supplied data buffer in place of a STREAMS data buffer. It calls allocb(D3DK) to get a message and data block header only. The user-supplied data buffer, pointed to by *base*, is used as the data buffer for the message.

The free_rtn structure is referenced by the dp_freep member of the datab structure. When freeb(D3DK) is called to free the message, the driver's message freeing routine (referenced through the free_rtn structure) is called, with arguments, to free the data buffer.

The free_rtn structure has the following declaration:

```
struct free_rtn {
    void (*free_func)();  /* user's freeing routine */
    char *free_arg;       /* arguments to free_func() */
}
typedef struct free_rtn frtn_t;
```

Instead of requiring a specific number of arguments, the free_arg field is defined of type char *. This way, the driver can pass a pointer to a structure if more than one argument is needed.

NOTE: The free_func function must be defined in kernel space, should be declared void and accept one argument. It has no user context and must not sleep.

RETURN VALUE
On success, a pointer to the newly allocated message block is returned. On failure, NULL is returned.

LEVEL
Base or Interrupt

SEE ALSO
allocb(D3DK), freeb(D3DK), datab(D4DK), free_rtn(D4DK)

esbbcall(D3DK)

NAME
esbbcall – call function when buffer is available

SYNOPSIS
```
#include <sys/stream.h>
```
mblk_t *esbbcall(int *pri,* int *func,* long *arg*);

ARGUMENTS
pri Priority of allocation request (to be used by allocb(D3DK) function, called by esbbcall)

func Function to be called when buffer becomes available.

arg Argument to *func*.

DESCRIPTION
esbbcall, like bufcall(D3DK), serves as a timeout(D3DK) call of indeterminate length. If esballoc(D3DK) is unable to allocate a message and data block header to go with its externally supplied data buffer, esbbcall can be used to schedule the routine *func*, to be called with the argument *arg* when a buffer becomes available. *func* may be a routine that calls esbbcall or it may be another kernel function.

RETURN VALUE
On success, 1 is returned. On failure, 0 is returned.

LEVEL
Base or Interrupt

SEE ALSO
BCI Driver Development Guide, Chapter 7, "STREAMS"

allocb(D3DK), bufcall(D3DK), datab(D4DK), esballoc(D3DK)

etoimajor (D3D) etoimajor (D3D)

NAME
etoimajor – convert external to internal major device number

SYNOPSIS
#include <sys/types.h>
#include <sys/ddi.h>

int etoimajor(major_t *emaj*);

ARGUMENT
emaj   An external major number.

DESCRIPTION
etoimajor converts the external major number (*emaj*) to an internal major number.

RETURN VALUE
etoimajor returns the internal major number or NODEV if the external major number exceeds the **bdevsw** and **cdevsw** count.

LEVEL
Base or Interrupt

SEE ALSO
getemajor(D3D), geteminor(D3D), getmajor(D3DK), getminor(D3DK), itoemajor(D3D), makedevice(D3DK)

flushband (D3DK) flushband (D3DK)

NAME
flushband – flush messages for a specified priority band

SYNOPSIS
```
#include <sys/stream.h>
```
void flushband(queue_t *q*, unsigned char *pri*, int *flag*);

ARGUMENTS
q   Pointer to the queue.

pri   Priority of messages to be flushed.

flag   Valid *flag* values are:

     FLUSHDATA   Flush only data messages (types M_DATA, M_DELAY, M_PROTO, and M_PCPROTO).

     FLUSHALL   Flush all messages.

DESCRIPTION
The flushband function flushes messages associated with the priority band specified by *pri*. If *pri* is 0, only normal and high priority messages are flushed. Otherwise, messages are flushed from the band *pri* according to the value of *flag*.

RETURN VALUE
None

LEVEL
Base or Interrupt

SEE ALSO
BCI Driver Development Guide, Chapter 7, "STREAMS"

flushq(D3DK)

flushq (D3DK)

NAME
flushq – remove messages from a queue

SYNOPSIS
```
#include <sys/stream.h>
```
void flushq(queue_t *q, int *flag*);

ARGUMENTS
q Pointer to the queue to be flushed.

flag Valid *flag* values are:

FLUSHDATA Flush only data messages (types M_DATA, M_DELAY, M_PROTO, and M_PCPROTO).

FLUSHALL Flush all messages.

DESCRIPTION
flushq frees messages and their associated data structures by calling freemsg(D3DK). If the queue's count falls below the low water mark and QWANTW is set, the nearest upstream service procedure is enabled.

RETURN VALUE
None

LEVEL
Base or Interrupt

SEE ALSO
BCI Driver Development Guide, Chapter 7, "STREAMS"

freemsg(D3DK), putq(D3DK)

EXAMPLE
This example depicts the canonical flushing code for STREAMS modules. The module has a write service procedure and potentially has messages on the queue. If it receives an M_FLUSH message, and if the FLUSHR bit is on in the first byte of the message (line 10), then the read queue is flushed (line 11). If the FLUSHW bit is on (line 12), then the write queue is flushed (line 13). Then the message is passed along to the next entity in the stream (line 14). See the example for qreply(D3DK) for the canonical flushing code for drivers.

```
1   /*
2    * Module write-side put procedure.
3    */
4   xxxwput(q, mp)
5       queue_t *q;
6       mblk_t *mp;
7   {
8       switch(mp->b_datap->db_type) {
9       case M_FLUSH:
10          if (*mp->b_rptr & FLUSHR)
11              flushq(RD(q), FLUSHALL);
12          if (*mp->b_rptr & FLUSHW)
13              flushq(q, FLUSHALL);
14          putnext(q, mp);
```

```
15            break;
                ...
16     }
17  }
```

freeb (D3DK)

NAME
freeb – free a message block

SYNOPSIS
```
#include <sys/stream.h>

void freeb(mblk_t *bp);
```

ARGUMENTS
bp   Pointer to the message block to be deallocated. `mblk_t` is an instance of the `msgb`(D4DK) structure.

DESCRIPTION
`freeb` deallocates a message block. If the reference count of the `db_ref` member of the `datab`(D4DK) structure is greater than 1, `freeb` decrements the count. If `db_ref` equals 1, it deallocates the message block and the corresponding data block and buffer.

If the data buffer to be freed was allocated with the `esballoc`(D3DK) function, the buffer may be a non-STREAMS resource. In that case, the driver must be notified that the attached data buffer needs to be freed, and run its own freeing routine. To make this process independent of the driver used in the stream, `freeb` finds the `free_rtn`(D4DK) structure associated with the buffer. The `free_rtn`(D4DK) structure contains a pointer to the driver-dependent routine, which releases the buffer. Once this is accomplished, `freeb` releases the STREAMS resources associated with the buffer.

RETURN VALUE
None

LEVEL
Base or Interrupt

SEE ALSO
BCI Driver Development Guide, Chapter 7, "STREAMS"

`allocb`(D3DK), `dupb`(D3DK), `esballoc`(D3DK), `free_rtn`(D4DK)

EXAMPLE
See the `copyb`(D3DK) function page for an example of `freeb`.

freemsg (D3DK)

NAME
freemsg – free all message blocks in a message

SYNOPSIS
#include <sys/stream.h>

int freemsg(mblk_t *mp);

ARGUMENT
mp Pointer to the message blocks to be deallocated. mblk_t is an instance of the msgb(D4DK) structure.

DESCRIPTION
freemsg calls freeb(D3DK) to free all message and data blocks associated with the message pointed to by *mp*.

RETURN VALUE
None

LEVEL
Base or Interrupt

SEE ALSO
BCI Driver Development Guide, Chapter 7, "STREAMS"

freeb(D3DK)

EXAMPLE
See the copymsg(D3DK) function page for an example of freemsg.

freerbuf(D3DK) freerbuf(D3DK)

NAME
freerbuf – free a raw buffer header

SYNOPSIS
```
#include <sys/buf.h>
#include <sys/ddi.h>

void freerbuf(struct buf *bp);
```

ARGUMENTS
bp   Pointer to a previously allocated buffer header structure.

DESCRIPTION
freerbuf frees a raw buffer header previously allocated by **getrbuf**(D3DK). This function does not sleep and so may be called from an interrupt routine.

RETURN VALUE
None

LEVEL
Base or Interrupt

SEE ALSO
getrbuf(D3DK), kmem_alloc(D3DK), kmem_free(D3DK), kmem_zalloc(D3DK)

getemajor (D3D) getemajor (D3D)

NAME
getemajor – get external major device number

SYNOPSIS
```
#include <sys/types.h>
#include <sys/ddi.h>
```
major_t getemajor(dev_t *dev*);

ARGUMENT
dev   An external device number (contains both the major and minor number).

DESCRIPTION
getemajor returns the external major number given a device number, *dev*.

RETURN VALUE
The external major number.

LEVEL
Base or Interrupt

SEE ALSO
geteminor(D3D), etoimajor(D3D), getmajor(D3DK), makedevice(D3DK), getminor(D3DK)

geteminor(D3D) geteminor(D3D)

NAME
geteminor – get external minor device number

SYNOPSIS
```
#include <sys/types.h>
#include <sys/ddi.h>
```
minor_t geteminor(dev_t *dev*);

ARGUMENT
dev   External device number.

DESCRIPTION
geteminor returns the external minor number given a device number, *dev*.

RETURN VALUE
The external minor number.

LEVEL
Base or Interrupt

SEE ALSO
getemajor(D3D), etoimajor(D3D), getmajor(D3DK), makedevice(D3DK), getminor(D3DK)

NAME

geterror – return I/O error

SYNOPSIS

```
#include <sys/types.h>
#include <sys/buf.h>

int geterror(struct buf *bp);
```

ARGUMENT

bp   Pointer to the block interface buffer structure defined in `buf.h`.

DESCRIPTION

`geterror` is called to retrieve the error number from the error field of the buffer header structure.

RETURN VALUE

An error number indicating the error condition of the I/O request is returned. If the I/O requested is completed successfully, 0 is returned.

LEVEL

Base or Interrupt

SEE ALSO

buf(D4DK)

getmajor (D3DK)

NAME
getmajor – get major or internal major device number

SYNOPSIS
```
#include <sys/types.h>
#include <sys/mkdev.h>
#include <sys/ddi.h>

major_t getmajor(dev_t dev);
```

ARGUMENT
dev   Device number.

DESCRIPTION
The `getmajor` function extracts either the major number or the internal major number from a device number. For the 3B2, `getmajor` returns the internal major number. For architectures that do not make a distinction between internal and external major numbers, `getmajor` returns the major number.

RETURN VALUE
The major number or internal major number.

NOTE: No validty checking is performed. If *dev* is invalid, an invalid number is returned.

LEVEL
Base or Interrupt

SEE ALSO
BCI Driver Development Guide, Chapter 3, "Drivers in the UNIX Operating System"

makedevice(D3DK), getminor(D3DK)

EXAMPLE
The following example shows both the `getmajor` and `getminor(D3DK)` functions used in a debug `cmn_err(D3DK)` statement to return the major and minor numbers for the device supported by the driver. This example is 3B2 specific.

```
dev_t dev;

#ifdef DEBUG
cmn_err(CE_NOTE,"Driver Started.  Internal Major# = %d,
    Internal Minor# = %d", getmajor(dev), getminor(dev));
#endif
```

getminor (D3DK)

NAME
getminor – get minor or internal minor device number

SYNOPSIS
```
#include <sys/types.h>
#include <sys/mkdev.h>
#include <sys/ddi.h>
```
minor_t getminor(dev_t *dev*);

ARGUMENT
dev   Device number.

DESCRIPTION
The `getminor` function extracts either the minor number or the internal minor number from a device number. For the 3B2, `getminor` returns the internal minor number. For architectures that do not make a distinction between internal and external minor numbers, `getminor` returns the minor number.

RETURN VALUE
The minor number or internal minor number.

NOTE: No validty checking is performed. If *dev* is invalid, an invalid number is returned.

LEVEL
Base or Interrupt

SEE ALSO
BCI Driver Development Guide, Chapter 3, "Drivers in the UNIX Operating System"

getmajor(D3DK), makedevice(D3DK)

getq (D3DK)

NAME
getq – get the next message from a queue

SYNOPSIS
```
#include <sys/stream.h>

mblk_t *getq(queue_t *q);
```

ARGUMENTS
q   Pointer to the queue from which the message is to be retrieved.

DESCRIPTION
getq is used by a service (srv(D2DK)) routine to retrieve its enqueued messages.

A module or driver may include a service routine to process enqueued messages. Once the STREAMS scheduler calls **srv** it must process all enqueued messages, unless prevented by flow control. getq gets the next available message from the top of the queue pointed to by *q*. It should be called in a **while** loop that should be exited only when there are no more messages.

getq turns the QWANTR flag off when a queue is being read, and turns QWANTR on when there are no more messages. When QWANTW is set it means an attempt has been made to write to the queue while it was blocked by flow control. If this is the case, getq back-enables (restarts) the service routine once it falls below the low water mark.

RETURN VALUE
If there is a message to retrieve, getq returns a pointer to it. If no message is queued, getq returns a NULL pointer.

LEVEL
Base or Interrupt

SEE ALSO
BCI Driver Development Guide, Chapter 7, "STREAMS"

STREAMS Programmer's Guide, Chapter 5, "Messages"

bcanput(D3DK), canput(D3DK), putbq(D3DK), putq(D3DK), qenable(D3DK), srv(D2DK)

EXAMPLE
See the dupb(D3DK) function page for an example of getq.

getrbuf(D3DK)   **getrbuf(D3DK)**

NAME
   getrbuf – get a raw buffer header

SYNOPSIS
   #include <sys/buf.h>
   #include <sys/kmem.h>
   #include <sys/ddi.h>

   struct buf *getrbuf(long *sleepflag*);

ARGUMENT
   sleepflag   Indicates whether driver should sleep for free space.

DESCRIPTION
   getrbuf allocates the space for a buffer header to the caller. It is used in cases where a block driver is performing raw (character interface) I/O and needs to set up a buffer header that is not associated with the buffer cache.

   getrbuf calls kmem_alloc(D3DK) to perform the memory allocation. kmem_alloc requires the information included in the *sleepflag* argument. If *sleepflag* is set to KM_SLEEP, the driver may sleep until the space is freed up. If *sleepflag* is set to KM_NOSLEEP, the driver will not sleep. In either case, a pointer to the allocated space is returned or NULL to indicate that no space was available.

RETURN VALUE
   A pointer to the allocated buffer header, or NULL if no space is available.

LEVEL
   Base or Interrupt (must not sleep if calling from interrupt routine)

SEE ALSO
   freerbuf(D3DK), kmem_alloc(D3DK), kmem_free(D3DK)

getvec(D3D)   **getvec(D3D)**

NAME

getvec – get an interrupt vector for a virtual feature card address

SYNOPSIS

unsigned char getvec(long *baddr*);

ARGUMENTS

baddr   A virtual feature card address.

DESCRIPTION

getvec returns an interrupt vector for a specified virtual feature card address. getvec is used in an init(D2D) routine. NOTE: If the feature card address is 0, a divide-by-zero error can occur.

RETURN VALUE

Under all conditions, an unsigned char numeric value is returned. The only abnormal return value is a number not logical for the circumstances.

LEVEL

Base Only (Do not call from an interrupt routine)

EXAMPLE

With a 3B2 computer, each device that generates an interrupt must be given an interrupt vector location code. During system initialization, the driver init routine gets the interrupt vector location code (line 17) and stores the code in a predefined address on the interface card (an address on the card in the range of 0x0 to 0x200000 can be defined to hold the code).

When a device generates an interrupt, the interface card presents the code to the CPU, which uses it to locate the interrupt handling routine(s) of the driver.

```
1   struct  device  {              /* physical device registers layout  */
2           char    reserve[4];    /* reserve space on card             */
3           ushort  control;       /* physical device control word      */
4           char    status;        /* physical device status word       */
5           char    ivec_num;      /* device interrupt vector number in */
6                                  /* 0xf0; subdevice reporting in 0x0f */
7           paddr_t addr;          /* address of data to be read/written */
8           int     count;         /* amount of data to be read/written */
9   }; /* end device */
10
11  extern struct device *xx_addr[]; /* physical dev registers location */
12
13  xx_init()
14  {
15                                  /* get device register struct */
16      register struct device *rp = xx_addr[0];
17      rp->ivec_num = getvec(xx_addr[0]); /* get interrupt vector code */
18
19  } /* end xx_init */
```

hat_getkpfnum (D3K)　　　　　　　　　　　　　　　　　　　　　　　　**hat_getkpfnum (D3K)**

NAME
hat_getkpfnum – get page frame number for kernel address

SYNOPSIS
```
#include <sys/vm.h>
#include <sys/types.h>

u_int hat_getkpfnum(caddr_t addr);
```

ARGUMENT
addr　　The kernel virtual address for which the page frame number is to be returned.

DESCRIPTION
Drivers implementing the mmap(D2K) entry point must return −1 (for error) or the page frame number corresponding to the virtual address of the device memory *addr*. This frame number can be obtained by a call to hat_getkpfnum.

RETURN VALUE
The page frame number corresponding to virtual address *addr*. There is no special error return value; invalid addresses will produce meaningless return values.

LEVEL
Base or interrupt. Although there is no reason why hat_getkpfnum cannot be called at interrupt level, there is no need since it only needs to be called from mmap(D2K).

SEE ALSO
mmap(D2K), page_numtopp(D2DK), page_pptonum(D2DK)

hdeeqd (D3D)

NAME
hdeeqd – initialize hard disk error logging

SYNOPSIS
```
#include <sys/types.h>
#include <sys/hdelog.h>
#include <sys/mkdev.h>
```
int hdeeqd(o_dev_t *dev*, daddr_t *pdsno*, short *edtyp*);

ARGUMENTS
dev External device number (contains both the major number and the minor number). The driver must call the `cmpdev` macro (defined in `mkdev.h`) to compress the device number.

pdsno Physical description sector

edtyp Error device type. The valid values are

EQD_EFC	external floppy controller
EQD_EHDC	external hard disk controller
EQD_ID	integral disk drive
EQD_IF	integral floppy disk drive
EQD_TAPE	cartridge tape drive

DESCRIPTION
hdeeqd initializes information in the hard disk error logging table for the device specified by *dev*. This function is called once per device.

NOTE: This function is not part of the default set of kernel functions. Ensure that the HDE bootable object module is placed in the /boot directory.

RETURN VALUE
Under all conditions, a 0 is returned. However, internal errors can occur in **hdeeqd** causing a warning message to display on the console. Errors occur in the following conditions:

The internal major device number is greater than or equal to the number of the controllers, called `cdevcnt`, which is assigned by `lboot` when the operating system is loaded. The message is

```
WARNING: hdeeqd: major(ddev) = int-major (>=cdevcnt)
```

int-major is the internal major device number.

The count of used disk slots in the error logging table exceeds the number of available slots. The message is

```
WARNING: Too few HDE equipped slots
bad block handling skipped for maj/min = ext-maj, ext-min
```

ext-maj and *ext-min* are the external major and minor numbers.

LEVEL
Base or Interrupt

hdeeqd (D3D)   hdeeqd (D3D)

SEE ALSO
BCI Driver Development Guide, Chapter 12, "Error Reporting"
hdelog(D3D), hdedata(D4D)

EXAMPLE
When a device is opened for the first time, the driver open(D2DK) or init(D2D) routines (open in this example) must identify the device and set up controlling information about the device. In this example, the information is kept on a controlling sector on the disk. If the controlling sector does not exist, the information is encoded as a `static` table in the driver.

```
 1   #define XX_CNTLBLKNO    0       /* controlling sector block number  */
 2   struct  device {                /* physical device registers layout */
 3           char    reserve[4];     /* reserve space on card            */
 4           ushort  control;        /* physical device control word     */
 5           char    status;         /* physical device status word      */
 6           char    ivec_num;       /* device interrupt vector number in */
 7                                   /* 0xf0; subdevice reporting in 0x0f */
 8           paddr_t addr;           /* data address to be read/written  */
 9           int     count;          /* amount of data to be read/written */
10   }; /* end device */
11   struct xx_    {                 /* logical device structure         */
12           struct buf     *xx_head; /* I/O buffer queue head pointer   */
13           struct buf     *xx_tail; /* I/O buffer queue tail pointer   */
14           short           xx_flag; /* logical status flag             */
15           struct hdedata xx_edata; /* disk error log error record     */
16           struct iostat  xx_stat;  /* unit I/O statistics for         */
17                          /* establishing an error rate during error logging */
18   }; /* end xx_ */
19
20   struct xx_info {                 /* information on control sector   */
21           long    xx_id;           /* disk device id code             */
22           long    xx_cyl;          /* total number of cylinders       */
23           long    xx_trk;          /* number of tracks per cylinder   */
24           long    xx_sec;          /* number of sectors per track     */
25           char    xx_serial[12];   /* device serial number            */
26   }; /* end xx_info */
27
28   extern struct xx_    xx_devtab[]; /* logical device structures table */
29   extern struct device *xx_addr[];  /* physical dev registers location */
30   extern struct xx_info xx_info[];  /* device control information      */
31   extern int           xx_cnt;      /* number of devices               */
     . . .
32   xx_open(dev, flag, otyp, crp)
33           dev_t   *dev;
34           int     flag, otype;
35           struct cred *crp;
36   {
37       register struct xx_     *dp;
38       register struct device  *rp;
```

```
39      register int unit;
        . . .
40      unit = getminor(dev) >> 4;           /* get drive unit number */
41      dp   = &xx_devtab[unit];      /* get logical device information */
42  if ((dp->xx_flag & XX_OPEN) == 0) { /* if first time device opened */
43      register struct buf *bp;
44      hdeeqd(cmpdev(dev), XX_CNTLBLKNO, EQD_ID); /* initialize error logging */
45      bp = kmem_alloc(1024, KM_NOSLEEP); /* get control sector buffer */
46      bp->b_flags = B_READ;                /* set up buffer to read */
47      bp->b_blkno = XX_CNTLBLKNO;          /* control sector from disk */
48      bp->b_count = 512;
49      bp->b_dev = dev;
50      xx_strategy(bp);                     /* read control sector */
51      biowait(bp);                         /* wait for read to complete */
52      if ((bp->b_flags & B_ERROR) != 0 ) {
53              /* if data error occurred, display message on console */
54          xx_print(dev, "xx_open: cannot read control sector");
55      } else {            /* copy control sector data to info table */
56          bcopy(bp->b_un.b_addr, &xx_info[unit], sizeof(struct xx_info));
57          hdeeqd(cmpdev(dev), XX_CNTLBLKNO, EQD_ID);   /* start error logging */
58          dp->flag |= XX_OPEN;             /* indicate device open    */
59      } /* endif */
60      brelse(bp);                          /* release system buffer   */
61  } /* endif */
```

If this is the first open, **hdeeqd** (line 44) is used to initiate error logging for the device. A system buffer is allocated (line 45) and the driver reads the controlling sector from the **xx_strategy** routine (line 50). If an error occurred on the read attempt, an error message is displayed (line 54) and an error condition is returned. Otherwise, the driver saves information from the controlling sector with **bcopy** (line 56) and indicates the device has been opened. Finally, the system buffer is released (line 60).

hdelog (D3D)   **hdelog (D3D)**

NAME
hdelog – log hard disk error

SYNOPSIS
```
#include <sys/types.h>
#include <sys/hdelog.h>
#include <sys/mkdev.h>

int hdelog(struct hdedata *eptr);
```

ARGUMENT
eptr   Pointer to the hdedata(D4D) structure defined in sys/hdelog.h. The driver developer places information in the structure before hdelog is called.

DESCRIPTION
hdelog logs a hard disk error in the error logging queue and displays a warning message on the console to alert the operator to the problem.

The console message is

    WARNING: *severity readtype* **hard disk error:**
    maj/min = *external-major-num, external-minor-num*

where *severity* is "marginal" or "unreadable", and *readtype* is "CRC" (cyclic redundancy check) or "ECC" (error check and correction).

hdeeqd(D3D) must be called once before this function to initialize error logging. hdelog logs disk drive media errors. **NOTE:** This function is not part of the default kernel. Ensure that the HDE bootable object module is placed in the /boot directory.

Before calling this function, values must be assigned to the hdedata(D4D) structure. These members include the device number; the disk pack serial number; the physical block address; the type of read operation CRC or ECC; whether the error is marginal or whether the disk is unreadable; the number of unreadable tries; the bit width of the corrected error; and a time stamp.

RETURN VALUE
Under all conditions, a 0 is returned. However, an internal error can occur in hdelog causing a warning message to display on the console. This error occurs when the error logging table is full. In this case, the usual disk error warning message is prefaced with

    WARNING: HDE queue full, following report not logged

LEVEL
Base or Interrupt

SEE ALSO
BCI Driver Development Guide, Chapter 12, "Error Reporting"

hdeeqd(D3D), hdedata(D4D)

EXAMPLE
A driver interrupt routine must check for data transfer errors (called data checks). When a data check occurs (reported by the device in the status or error register), the driver determines if there have been sufficient attempts to resolve the error.

hdelog (D3D)

If so, the driver abandons the I/O request by marking the buffer as being in error, logging an unresolved error (line 60), and marking the I/O operation complete (line 61). When an error persists in spite of multiple attempts to resolve it, the driver logs marginal errors (line 75) and attempts the I/O operation again. The driver may try to resolve the error with software by using the error correction bits in an error check and correction (ECC) register. See hdedata(D4D) for a description of the xx_edata structure shown in this example line 17).

```
 1  struct  device   {
 2                                      /* layout of physical device regs */
 3          char      reserve[4];       /* reserve space on card          */
 4          ushort    control;          /* physical device control word   */
 5          char      status;           /* physical device status word    */
 6          char      ivec_num;         /* device interrupt vector no. in */
 7                                      /* 0xf0; subdevice in 0x0f        */
 8          paddr_t   addr;             /* address of data read/written   */
 9          int       count;            /* amount of data read/written    */
10  }; /* end device */
11
12  struct xx_ {
13                                      /* logical device structure       */
14          struct buf     *xx_head;    /* I/O buffer queue head pointer  */
15          struct buf     *xx_tail;    /* I/O buffer queue tail pointer  */
16          short          xx_flag;     /* logical status flag            */
17          struct hdedata xx_edata;    /* hard disk error record         */
18          struct iostat  xx_stat;     /* unit I/O stats for setting an  */
19                                      /* error rate during error logging*/
20  }; /* end xx_ */
21
22  struct xx_info  {
23                                      /* information on disk control sector */
24          long     xx_id;             /* device id code                 */
25          long     xx_cyl;            /* total number of cylinders      */
26          long     xx_trk;            /* number of tracks per cylinder  */
27          long     xx_sec;            /* number of sectors per track    */
28          char     xx_serial[12];     /* device serial number           */
29  }; /* end xx_info */
30  extern struct xx_      xx_devtab[];/* logical dev structures table    */
31  extern struct device *xx_addr[];    /* physical dev register location */
32  extern struct xx_info xx_info[];    /* device control information     */
33  extern int             xx_cnt;      /* number of devices              */
34  xx_int(board)
35          int  board;
36  {                                                 /* get dev registers */
37    register struct device *rp = xx_addr[board];
38    register struct xx_    *dp;
39    register struct buf    *bp;
40    register int            unit;
41
42    unit = (board << 4) | (rp->ivec_num & 0xf);     /* make unit number */
```

hdelog (D3D)

```
43      dp = &xx_devtab[unit];
44      if ((rp->status & DATACHK) != 0) {
45                                      /* if data check error occurred */
46         if (++dp->xx_edata.badrtcnt > XX_MAXTRY) {   /* if sufficient */
47             /* attempts have been made, then abandon the I/O request */
48             bp = dp->xx_head;            /* get buffer from I/O queue */
49             dp->xx_head = bp->av_forw; /* remove buffer from I/O queue */
50             bp->b_flags |= B_ERROR;   /* mark buffer as being in error */
51             bp->b_error = EIO;           /* supply error condition */
52                     /* supply information needed for error logging */
53             dp->xx_edata.diskdev = cmpdev(bp->b_dev);  /* device number */
54             dp->xx_edata.blkaddr = bp->b_blkno;   /* block no. in error */
55             dp->xx_edata.readtype = HDEECC;  /* error type: error check */
56             dp->xx_edata.severity = HDEUNRD;  /* data was unreadable    */
57             dp->xx_edata.bitwidth = 0;
58             dp->xx_edata.timestmp = time;  /* time recording occurred */
59             bcopy(dp->xx_edata.dskserno, xx_info[unit].serial, 12);
60             hdelog(&dp->xx_edata);       /* log abandoned I/O operations*/
61             biodone(bp);                 /* mark I/O operation complete */
62
63         } else if(dp->xx_edata.badrtcnt > 1) {/* if more than one retry */
64                                              /* log error as marginal */
65             bp = dp->xx_head;  /* get buffer from I/O queue but leave on */
66                        /* I/O queue so that I/O operation is repeated */
67             /* supply information needed for error logging */
68             dp->xx_edata.diskdev = cmpdev(bp->b_dev);   /* device number */
69             dp->xx_edata.blkaddr = bp->b_blkno;   /* error block number */
70             dp->xx_edata.readtype = HDEECC;   /* err. type: error check */
71             dp->xx_edata.severity = HDEMARG;        /* marginal error */
72             dp->xx_edata.bitwidth = 0;
73             dp->xx_edata.timestmp = time;  /* time recording occurred */
74             bcopy(dp->xx_edata.dskserno, xx_info[unit].serial, 12);
75             hdelog(&dp->xx_edata);             /* log data check error */
76         } /* endif */
77      } /* endif */
78   }
```

insq (D3DK)

NAME
insq – insert a message into a queue

SYNOPSIS
```
#include <sys/stream.h>
```
int insq(queue_t *q, mblk_t *emp, mblk_t *nmp);

ARGUMENTS
q Pointer to the queue containing message *emp*.

emp Enqueued message before which the new message is to be inserted (mblk_t is an instance of the msgb(D4DK) structure).

nmp Message to be inserted.

DESCRIPTION
insq inserts a message into a queue. The message to be inserted, *nmp*, is placed in *q* immediately before the message *emp*. If *emp* is NULL, the new message is placed at the end of the queue. The queue class of the new message is ignored. All flow control parameters are updated. The service procedure is enabled unless QNOENB is set.

CAUTION: If *emp* is non-NULL, it must point to a message on *q* or a system panic could result.

RETURN VALUE
insq returns 1 on success, and 0 on failure.

LEVEL
Base or Interrupt

SEE ALSO
BCI Driver Development Guide, Chapter 7, "STREAMS"

EXAMPLE
This routine illustrates the steps a transport provider may take to place expedited data ahead of normal data on a queue (assume all M_DATA messages are converted into M_PROTO T_DATA_REQ messages). Normal T_DATA_REQ messages are just placed on the end of the queue (line 14). However, expedited T_EXDATA_REQ messages are inserted before any normal messages already on the queue (line 28). If there are no normal messages on the queue, bp will be NULL and we will fall out of the for loop (line 21). insq will act like putq(D3DK) in this case.

```
1   #include <sys/tihdr.h>
2
3   xxxwput(q, mp)
4       queue_t *q;
5       mblk_t *mp;
6   {
7       union T_primitives *tp;
8
9       switch (mp->b_datap->db_type) {
10      case M_PROTO:
11              tp = (union T_primitives *)mp->b_rptr;
```

```
12              switch (tp->type) {
13              case T_DATA_REQ:
14                      putq(q, mp);
15                      break;
16
17              case T_EXDATA_REQ:
19                      mblk_t *bp;
20                      union T_primitives *ntp;
21
22                      for (bp = q->q_first; bp; bp = bp->b_next) {
23                         if (bp->b_datap->db_type == M_PROTO) {
24                           ntp = (union T_primitives *)bp->b_rptr;
25                           if (ntp->type != T_EXDATA_REQ)
26                              break;
27                         }
28                      }
29                      insq(q, bp, mp);
30                      break;
        . . .
32                 }
33       }
34  }
```

itoemajor (D3D)

NAME
itoemajor – convert internal to external major device number

SYNOPSIS
```
#include <sys/types.h>
#include <sys/ddi.h>

int itoemajor(major_t imaj, int prevemaj);
```

ARGUMENTS
imaj An internal major number.

prevemaj Most recently obtained external major number (or **NODEV**, if this is the first time the function has been called).

DESCRIPTION
itoemajor converts the internal major number to the external major number. The external-to-internal major number mapping is many-to-one, and so any internal major number may correspond to more than one external major number. By repeatedly invoking this function and passing the most recent external major number obtained, the driver can obtain all possible external major number values.

RETURN VALUE
External major number, or **NODEV**, if all have been searched

LEVEL
Base or Interrupt

SEE ALSO
getemajor(D3D), geteminor(D3D), etoimajor(D3D), getmajor(D3DK), getminor(D3DK), makedevice(D3DK)

kmem_alloc(D3DK) kmem_alloc(D3DK)

NAME
kmem_alloc – allocate space from kernel free memory

SYNOPSIS
```
#include <sys/types.h>
#include <sys/kmem.h>

_VOID *kmem_alloc(size_t size, int flag);
```

ARGUMENTS
size Number of bytes to allocate.

flag Determines if caller will sleep to wait for free space. Possible flags are KM_SLEEP to sleep while waiting for free space, and KM_NOSLEEP to return NULL if space is not available.

DESCRIPTION
The kmem_alloc function allocates a specified amount of kernel memory in bytes and returns a pointer to the allocated memory. The *flag* argument determines whether the function will sleep while waiting for free space to be released. If *flag* has KM_SLEEP set, the caller may sleep until free space is available. If *flag* has KM_NOSLEEP set and space is not available, NULL will be returned.

NOTE: Memory allocated by kmem_alloc is not paged. Available memory is therefore limited. Excessive use of this memory is likely to affect overall system performance.

RETURN VALUE
If successfull, kmem_alloc returns a pointer to the allocated space. NULL is returned if KM_NOSLEEP is set and memory cannot be allocated.

LEVEL
Base (interrupt only if KM_NOSLEEP is set in *flag*)

SEE ALSO
freerbuf(D3DK), getrbuf(D3DK), kmem_free(D3DK), kmem_zalloc(D3DK), rmalloc(D3DK), rmfree(D3DK), rminit(D3DK), rmsetwant(D3DK), rmwant(D3DK)

kmem_free(D3DK)   kmem_free(D3DK)

NAME
   kmem_free – free previously allocated kernel memory

SYNOPSIS
   #include <sys/tpes.h>
   #include <sys/kmem.h>

   void kmem_free(_VOID *cp, size_t size);

ARGUMENTS
   cp   Address of the allocated storage from which to return size of allocated memory.

   size   Number of bytes to free (same number of bytes as allocated by kmem_alloc(D3DK) or kmem_zalloc(D3DK).

DESCRIPTION
   This function returns size of storage to kernel free space previously allocated by kmem_alloc(D3DK) or kmem_zalloc(D3DK). The cp and size values must specify exactly one complete area of allocated memory. One kmem_free call must correspond to one allocation.

RETURN VALUE
   Under all conditions, no value is returned.

LEVEL
   Base or Interrupt

SEE ALSO
   freerbuf(D3DK), getrbuf(D3DK), kmem_alloc(D3DK), kmem_zalloc(D3DK), rmalloc(D3DK), rmfree(D3DK), rminit(D3DK), rmsetwant(D3DK), rmwant(D3DK)

kmem_zalloc (D3DK)

NAME
kmem_zalloc – allocate and clear space from kernel free memory

SYNOPSIS
```
#include <sys/types.h>
#include <sys/kmem.h>

_VOID *kmem_zalloc(unsigned long size, unsigned long flag);
```

ARGUMENTS
size   Number of bytes to allocate.

flag   Determines if caller may sleep to wait for free space. Possible flags are KM_SLEEP to sleep while waiting for free space, and KM_NOSLEEP to return NULL if space is not available.

DESCRIPTION
This function allocates *size* of storage from kernel free space, clears it, and returns a pointer to the allocated memory. If *flag* has KM_SLEEP set, the caller may sleep until free space is available. If *flag* has KM_NOSLEEP set and space is not available, NULL will be returned.

NOTE: Memory allocated by kmem_zalloc is not paged. Available memory is therefore limited. Excessive use of this memory is likely to affect overall system performance.

RETURN VALUE
kmem_zalloc returns NULL if memory cannot be allocated. Otherwise, it returns a pointer to the allocated space.

LEVEL
Base (interrupt only if KM_NOSLEEP is set in *flag*)

SEE ALSO
freerbuf(D3DK), getrbuf(D3DK), kmem_alloc(D3DK), kmem_free(D3DK), rmalloc(D3DK), rmfree(D3DK), rminit(D3DK), rmsetwant(D3DK), rmwant(D3DK)

kvtophys(D3D)   **kvtophys(D3D)**

NAME

kvtophys – convert kernel virtual address to physical address

SYNOPSIS

```
#include <sys/types.h>
#include <sys/ddi.h>
```

paddr_t kvtophys(caddr_t *caddr*);

ARGUMENTS

caddr   Kernel virtual address to translate.

DESCRIPTION

This function returns the physical address equivalent of the specified kernel virtual address. The same functionality is provided in the **vtop**(D3D) function.

RETURN VALUE

kvtophys returns **NULL** if *caddr* is invalid; otherwise, a physical address is returned. **CAUTION:** If *caddr* is invalid, **kvtophys** could panic the system.

LEVEL

Base or Interrupt

SEE ALSO

vtop(D3D)

linkb (D3DK)

NAME
linkb – concatenate two message blocks

SYNOPSIS
```
#include <sys/stream.h>
```
void linkb(mblk_t *mp1, mblk_t *mp2);

ARGUMENTS
mp1 The message to which *mp2* is to be added. mblk_t is an instance of the msgb(D4DK) structure.

mp2 The message to be added.

DESCRIPTION
linkb creates a new message by adding *mp2* to the tail of *mp1*. The continuation pointer (b_cont) of the first message is set to point to the second message:

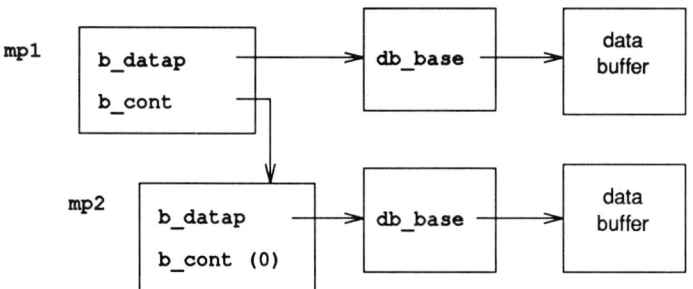

linkb(mp1, mp2);

RETURN VALUE
None

LEVEL
Base or Interrupt

SEE ALSO
BCI Driver Development Guide, Chapter 7, "STREAMS"

unlinkb(D3DK)

EXAMPLE
See the dupb(D3DK) function page for an example of linkb.

makedevice (D3DK)

NAME
makedevice – make device number from external major and minor

SYNOPSIS
```
#include <sys/types.h>
#include <sys/makedev.h>
#include <sys/ddi.h>
```
dev_t makedevice(major_t *majnum*, minor_t *minnum*);

ARGUMENTS
majnum   External major number.

minnum   External minor number.

DESCRIPTION
The **makedevice** function creates a device number from an external major and external minor device number. **makdevice** should be used to create device numbers so that additional overhead on the driver can be avoided, and so the driver will port easily to releases that treat device numbers differently.

RETURN VALUE
The device number, containing both the major number and the minor number, is returned. No validation of the external major or minor numbers is performed.

NOTE: The numbers returned by getmajor(D3DK) and getminor(D3DK) are not valid arguments to **makedevice** in systems where there is a distinction between internal and external numbers. The functions getemajor(D3D) and geteminor(D3D) should be used on those systems.

LEVEL
Base or Interrupt

SEE ALSO
BCI Driver Development Guide, Chapter 3, "Drivers in the UNIX Operating System"

getemajor(D3D), geteminor(D3D), getmajor(D3DK), getminor(D3DK)

EXAMPLE
In the following example **makedevice** creates device numbers for every device supported by the example init(D2D) routine. The init routine initializes each device by calling the xxx_dev_init() routine (line 8) with the device number for each device. The device numbers are created from the preconfigured major device number, XXMAJOR, and the range of valid minor numbers for the device.

```
1   xxxinit()
2   {
3        dev_t dev;
4        minor_t min;
5
6        for (min = 0; min < XXMAXMIN; min++) {
7             dev = makedevice(XXMAJOR, min);
8             xxx_dev_init(dev);
9        }
10  }
```

max (D3DK)

NAME
    max – return the larger of two integers

SYNOPSIS
    `int max(int` *int1*`, int` *int2*`);`

ARGUMENTS
    int1, *int2*   The integers to be compared.

DESCRIPTION
    max compares two integers and returns the larger of two.

RETURN VALUE
    The larger of the two numbers.

LEVEL
    Base or Interrupt

SEE ALSO
    min(D3DK)

NAME

min – return the lesser of two integers

SYNOPSIS

```
int min(int int1, int int2);
```

ARGUMENTS

int1, *int2*   The integers to be compared.

DESCRIPTION

min compares two integers and returns the lesser of the two.

RETURN VALUE

The lesser of the two integers.

LEVEL

Base or Interrupt

SEE ALSO

max(D3DK)

msgdsize (D3DK)

NAME
msgdsize – return the number of bytes in a message

SYNOPSIS
#include <sys/stream.h>

int msgdsize(mblk_t *mp);

ARGUMENT
mp   Message to be evaluated.

DESCRIPTION
msgdsize counts the number of bytes in a data message. Only bytes included in the data blocks of type M_DATA are included in the count.

RETURN VALUE
The number of data bytes in a message, expressed as an integer.

LEVEL
Base or Interrupt

SEE ALSO
BCI Driver Development Guide, Chapter 7, "STREAMS"

EXAMPLE
See the bufcall(D3DK) function page for an example of the msgdsize function.

NAME
noenable – prevent a queue from being scheduled

SYNOPSIS
    #include <sys/stream.h>
    #include <sys/ddi.h>

    void noenable(queue_t *q);

ARGUMENT
q   Pointer to the queue.

DESCRIPTION
The `noenable` function prevents the queue q from being scheduled for service by `insq`(D3DK), or by `putq`(D3DK) or `putbq`(D3DK) when enqueuing an ordinary priority message. The queue can be re-enabled with the `enableok`(D3DK) function.

RETURN VALUE
None

LEVEL
Base or Interrupt

SEE ALSO
BCI Driver Development Guide, Chapter 7, "STREAMS"

enableok(D3DK), insq(D3DK), putq(D3DK), putbq(D3DK), qenable(D3DK)

OTHERQ (D3DK)

NAME
OTHERQ – get pointer to queue's partner queue

SYNOPSIS
```
#include <sys/stream.h>
#include <sys/ddi.h>

queue_t *OTHERQ(queue_t *q);
```

ARGUMENT
q   Pointer to the queue.

DESCRIPTION
The OTHERQ function returns a pointer to the other of the two queue structures that make up a STREAMS module or driver. If *q* points to the read queue the write queue will be returned, and vice versa.

RETURN VALUE
OTHERQ returns a pointer to a queue's partner.

LEVEL
Base or Interrupt

SEE ALSO
BCI Driver Development Guide, Chapter 7, "STREAMS"

EXAMPLE
This routine sets the minimum packet size, the maximum packet size, the high water mark, and the low water mark for the read and write queues of a given module or driver. It is passed either one of the queues. This could be used if a module or driver wished to update its queue parameters dynamically.

```
1   void
2   set_q_params(q, min, max, hi, lo)
3       queue_t *q;
4       short min;
5       short max;
6       ushort hi;
7       ushort lo;
8   {
9       q->q_minpsz = min;
10      q->q_maxpsz = max;
11      q->q_hiwat = hi;
12      q->q_lowat = lo;
13      OTHERQ(q)->q_minpsz = min;
14      OTHERQ(q)->q_maxpsz = max;
15      OTHERQ(q)->q_hiwat = hi;
16      OTHERQ(q)->q_lowat = lo;
17  }
```

NAME

page_numtopp – convert page frame number to page structure

SYNOPSIS

```
#include <sys/types.h>
#include <vm/page.h>
```

`page_t page_numtopp(u_int` *pfn*`);`

ARGUMENT

pfn   The page frame number to be converted.

DESCRIPTION

page_numtopp converts a page frame number to its corresponding page structure.

RETURN VALUE

A pointer to the page structure is returned. If the page frame number is invalid, NULL is returned.

LEVEL

Base or Interrupt

SEE ALSO

page_pptonum(D3DK)

NAME

`page_pptonum` – convert page structure to page frame number

SYNOPSIS

```
#include <sys/types.h>
#include <vm/page.h>

u_int page_pptonum(page_t *pp);
```

ARGUMENT

pp Pointer to a `page` structure.

DESCRIPTION

`page_pptonum` is called to convert a `page` structure to its corresponding page frame number.

RETURN VALUE

The page frame number corresponding to the `page` structure is returned. No error is returned. If *pp* (the `page` structure address) is invalid, the system will panic.

LEVEL

Base or Interrupt

SEE ALSO,

page_numtopp(D3DK),

physiock(D3D)   **physiock(D3D)**

NAME
physiock – validate and issue raw I/O request

SYNOPSIS
```
#include<sys/types.h>
#include <sys/buf.h>
#include <sys/errno.h>
#include <sys/uio.h>
#include <sys/cred.h>

int physiock(int (*(strategy) (), struct buf *buf, dev_t dev,
    int rwflag, daddr_t nblocks, uio_t *uio_p);
```

ARGUMENTS
strategy   Address of the driver **strategy** routine.

buf   Pointer to the **buf** structure describing the I/O request. If set to **NULL**, then a buffer is allocated from the buffer pool and returned to the free list after the transfer completes.

dev   Device number.

rwflag   Flag indicating whether the access is a read (**B_READ**) or a write (**B_WRITE**). Note that **B_WRITE** cannot be directly tested as it is 0

nblocks   Number of blocks that a logical device can support, for example, a disk partition, or tape.

uio_p   Pointer to the **uio** structure that defines the user space of the I/O request.

DESCRIPTION
physiock is called by the character interface to block driver **read**(D2DK) and **write**(D2DK) routines to help perform unbuffered I/O while maintaining the buffer header as the interface structure.

physiock performs the following functions:

   verifies the requested transfer is valid by checking if the offset is at or past the end of the device

   sets up a buffer header describing the transfer

   faults pages in and locks the pages impacted by the I/O transfer so they can not be swapped out

   calls the driver **strategy**(D2DK) routine passed to it

   sleeps until the transfer is complete and is awakened by the **biodone**(D3DK) function in the driver's interrupt routine

   performs the necessary cleanup and updates, then returns to the driver routine

A transfer using **physiock** is considered valid if the specified data location exists on the device, and the user has specified a storage area that exists in user memory space.

physiock(D3D)   physiock(D3D)

RETURN VALUE

physiock returns 0 if the result is successful, the appropriate error number upon failure. physiock returns the ENXIO error (see *Appendix A* for more information) if an attempt is made to read beyond the end of the device. If a read is performed at the end of the device, 0 is returned. ENXIO is also returned if an attempt is made to write at the end of a device or beyond the end of the device. EFAULT is returned if user memory is not available. EAGAIN is returned if physiock could not lock pages for DMA.

LEVEL

Base Only (Do not call from an interrupt routine)

SEE ALSO

dma_pageio(D3D), strategy(D2DK)

EXAMPLE

```
 1   struct  dsize      {
 2           daddr_t nblocks;   /* disk partition block number */
 3           int     cyloff;    /* starting cylinder # of partition  */
 4   } DISKsizes[16] = {
 5
 6           20448,  21,    /* partition 0 = cyl 21-305   */
 7           12888,  126,   /*     "      1 = cyl 126-305 */
 8            9360,  175,   /*     "      2 = cyl 175-305 */
 9            7200,  205,   /*     "      3 = cyl 205-305 */
10            3600,  255,   /*     "      4 = cyl 255-305 */
11           21816,  3,     /*     "      5 = cyl 2-305   */
12           21888,  1,     /*     "      6 = cyl 1-305   */
13              72,  1,     /*     "      7 = cyl 1       */
14   };
15
16   DISKread(dev, uio_p, cred_p)  /* direct read request from block device */
17           dev_t   dev;
18           uio_t   *uio_p;
19           cred_t  *cred_p;
20   {
21           register int nblks;
22
23           /* get number of blocks in the partition */
24           nblks = DISKsizes[minor(dev) & 0x7].nblocks;
25
26           /*
27            * Check limits of read request.  If request is in
28            * the limits of the disk partition, schedule direct I/O.
29            */
30
31           physiock(DISKstrat, 0, dev, B_READ, nblks, uio_p);
32
33   } /* end DISKread */
34
35
```

```
36  DISKwrite(dev, uio_p, cred_p)   /* direct write request to block device */
36      dev_t   dev;
37      uio_t   *uio_p;
38      cred_t  *cred_p
39  {
40      register int nblks;
41
42      /* get number of blocks in the partition */
43      nblks = DISKsizes[minor(dev) & 0x7].nblocks;
44
45      /*
46       * Check limits of write request.  If request is in
47       * the limits of the disk partition, schedule direct I/O.
48       */
49
50      physiock(DISKstrat, 0, dev, B_WRITE, nblks, uio_p);
51
52  } /* end DISKwrite */
```

pollwakeup (D3DK)

NAME
pollwakeup – inform a process that an event has occurred

SYNOPSIS
```
#include <sys/poll.h>
```
void pollwakeup(struct pollhead *php, short event);

ARGUMENTS
php   Pointer to a pollhead structure.

event   Event to notify the process about.

DESCRIPTION
The pollwakeup function wakes a process waiting on the occurrence of an event. It should be called from a driver for each occurrence of an event. The pollhead structure will usually be associated with the driver's private data structure associated with the particular minor device where the event has occurred. See chpoll(D2DK) and poll(2) for more detail.

RETURN
None

LEVEL
Base or Interrupt

SEE ALSO
chpoll(D2DK), poll(2)

ptob (D3DK)

NAME
ptob – convert size in pages to size in bytes

SYNOPSIS
```
#include <sys/ddi.h>
```
unsigned long ptob(unsigned long *numpages*);

ARGUMENT
numpages   Size in number of pages to convert to size in bytes.

DESCRIPTION
This function returns the number of bytes that are contained in the specified number of pages. For example, if the page size is 2048, then `ptob(2)` returns 4096. `ptob(0)` returns 0.

RETURN VALUE
The return value is always the number of bytes in the specified number of pages. There are no invalid input values, and no checking will be performed for overflow in the case of a page count whose corresponding byte count cannot be represented by an `unsigned long`. Rather, the higher order bits will be ignored.

LEVEL
Base or interrupt

SEE ALSO
btop(D3DK), btopr(D3DK)

pullupmsg(D3DK)

NAME
pullupmsg – concatenate bytes in a message

SYNOPSIS
```
#include <sys/stream.h>
```

int pullupmsg(mblk_t *`mp`, int `len`);

ARGUMENTS
*mp   Pointer to the message whose blocks are to be concatenated. mblk_t is an instance of the msgb(D4DK) structure.

len   Number of bytes to concatenate.

DESCRIPTION
pullupmsg tries to combine multiple data blocks into a single block. pullupmsg concatenates and aligns the first *len* data bytes of the message pointed to by *mp*. If *len* equals -1, all data is concatenated. If *len* bytes of the same message type cannot be found, pullupmsg fails and returns 0.

RETURN VALUE
On success, 1 is returned; on failure, 0 is returned.

LEVEL
Base or Interrupt

SEE ALSO
BCI Driver Development Guide, Chapter 7, "STREAMS"

allocb(D3DK)

EXAMPLE
This is a driver write srv(D2DK) (service) routine for a device that does not support scatter/gather DMA. For all M_DATA messages, the data will be transferred to the device with DMA.

First, try to pull up the message into one message block with the pullupmsg function (line 12). If successful, the transfer can be accomplished in one DMA job. Otherwise, it must be done one message block at a time (lines 19–22). After the data has been transferred to the device, free the message and continue processing messages on the queue.

```
1   xxxwsrv(q)
2       queue_t *q;
3   {
4       mblk_t *mp;
5       mblk_t *tmp;
6       caddr_t dma_addr;
7       int dma_len;
8
9       while ((mp = getq(q)) != NULL) {
10          switch (mp->b_datap->db_type) {
11          case M_DATA:
12              if (pullupmsg(mp, -1)) {
13                  dma_addr = vtop(mp->b_rptr);
14                  dma_len = mp->b_wptr - mp->b_rptr;
```

pullupmsg (D3DK)

```
15                      xxx_do_dma(dma_addr, dma_len);
16                      freemsg(mp);
17                      break;
18              }
19              for (tmp = mp; tmp; tmp = tmp->b_cont) {
20                      dma_addr = vtop(tmp->b_rptr);
21                      dma_len = tmp->b_wptr - tmp->b_rptr;
22                      xxx_do_dma(dma_addr, dma_len);
23              }
24              freemsg(mp);
25              break;
          . . .
26              }
27          }
28      }
```

NAME

putbq – place a message at the head of a queue

SYNOPSIS

```
#include <sys/stream.h>
```

int putbq(queue_t *q, mblk_t *bp);

ARGUMENTS

q   Pointer to the queue.

bp   Pointer to the message block.

DESCRIPTION

putbq places a message at the beginning of the appropriate section of the message queue. There are always sections for high priority and ordinary messages. If other priority bands are used, each will have its own section of the queue, in priority band order, after high priority messages and before ordinary messages. putbq can be used only for ordinary and priority band messages. High priority messages are not subject to flow control, and so cannot be put back on the queue.

This function is usually called when bcanput(D3DK) or canput(D3DK) determines that the message cannot be passed on to the next stream component. The flow control parameters are updated to reflect the change in the queue's status. If QNOENB is not set, the service routine is enabled.

RETURN VALUE

putbq returns 1 on success and 0 on failure.

LEVEL

Base or Interrupt

SEE ALSO

BCI Driver Development Guide, Chapter 7, "STREAMS"

STREAMS Programmer's Guide, Chapter 5, "Messages"

bcanput(D3DK), canput(D3DK), getq(D3DK), putq(D3DK)

EXAMPLE

See the bufcall(D3DK) function page for an example of putbq.

putctl(D3DK) putctl(D3DK)

NAME
putctl – send a control message to a queue

SYNOPSIS
```
#include <sys/stream.h>
```
int putctl(queue_t *q, int type);

ARGUMENTS
q Queue to which the message is to be sent.

type Message type (must be control, not data type).

DESCRIPTION
putctl tests the *type* argument to make sure a data type has not been specified, and then attempts to allocate a message block. putctl fails if *type* is M_DATA, M_DELAY, M_PROTO, or M_PCPROTO, or if a message block cannot be allocated. If successful, putctl calls the put(D2DK) routine of the queue pointed to by *q*.

RETURN VALUE
On success, 1 is returned. If *type* is a data type, or if a message block cannot be allocated, 0 is returned.

LEVEL
Base or Interrupt

SEE ALSO
BCI Driver Development Guide, Chapter 7, "STREAMS"

datamsg(D3DK), putctl1(D3DK)

EXAMPLE
The send_ctl routine is used to pass control messages downstream. M_BREAK messages are handled with putctl (line 11). putctl1 (line 16) is used for M_DELAY messages, so that *parm* can be used to specify the length of the delay. In either case, if a message block cannot be allocated a variable recording the number of allocation failures is incremented (lines 12, 17). If an invalid message type is detected, cmn_err(D3DK) panics the system (line 21).

```
 1  void
 2  send_ctl(wrq, type, parm)
 3      queue_t *wrq;
 4      unchar type;
 5      unchar parm;
 6  {
 7      extern int num_alloc_fail;
 8
 9      switch (type) {
10      case M_BREAK:
11          if (!putctl(wrq->q_next, M_BREAK))
12              num_alloc_fail++;
13          break;
14
15      case M_DELAY:
16          if (!putctl1(wrq->q_next, M_DELAY, parm))
```

```
17                  num_alloc_fail++;
18            break;
19
20      default:
21            cmn_err(CE_PANIC, "send_ctl: bad message type passed");
22            break;
23      }
24  }
```

NAME

putctl1 – send a control message with a one-byte parameter to a queue

SYNOPSIS

```
#include <sys/stream.h>
```

int putctl1(queue_t *q, int *type*, int *p*);

ARGUMENTS

q   Queue to which the message is to be sent.

type Type of message.

p   One-byte parameter.

DESCRIPTION

putctl1, like putctl(D3DK), tests the *type* argument to make sure a data type has not been specified, and attempts to allocate a message block. The *p* parameter can be used, for example, to specify how long the delay will be when an M_DELAY message is being sent. putctl1 fails if type is M_DATA, M_PROTO, or M_PCPROTO, or if a mesage block cannot be allocated. If successful, putctl1 calls the put(D2DK) routine of the queue pointed to by *q*.

RETURN VALUE

On success, 1 is returned. 0 is returned if *type* is a data type, or if a message block cannot be allocated.

LEVEL

Base or Interrupt

SEE ALSO

BCI Driver Development Guide, Chapter 7, "STREAMS"

allocb(D3DK), datamsg(D3DK), putctl(D3DK)

EXAMPLE

See the putctl(D3DK) function page for an example of putctl1.

putnext (D3DK)

NAME
putnext – send a message to the next queue

SYNOPSIS
```
#include <sys/stream.h>
#include <sys/ddi.h>

int putnext(queue_t *q, mblk_t *mp);
```

ARGUMENTS
q   Pointer to the queue from which the message *mp* will be sent.

mp   Message to be passed.

DESCRIPTION
The `putnext` function is used to pass a message to the put(D2DK) routine of the next queue in the stream.

RETURN VALUE
None

LEVEL
Base or Interrupt

SEE ALSO
BCI Driver Development Guide, Chapter 7, "STREAMS"

EXAMPLE
See the `allocb`(D3DK) function page for an example of `putnext`.

putq(D3DK)

NAME
putq – put a message on a queue

SYNOPSIS
```
#include <sys/stream.h>

int putq(queue_t *q, mblk_t *bp);
```

ARGUMENTS
q Pointer to the queue to which the message is to be added.

bp Message to be put on the queue.

DESCRIPTION
putq is used to put messages on a driver's queue after the module's put routine has finished processing the message. The message is placed after any other messages of the same priority, and flow control parameters are updated. If QNOENB is not set, the service routine is enabled. If no processing is done, putq can be used as the module's put routine.

RETURN VALUE
putq returns 1 on success and 0 on failure.

LEVEL
Base or Interrupt

SEE ALSO
BCI Driver Development Guide, Chapter 7, "STREAMS"

putbq(D3DK), qenable(D3DK), rmvq(D3DK)

EXAMPLE
See the datamsg(D3DK) function page for an example of putq.

qenable(D3DK)

NAME
qenable – enable a queue

SYNOPSIS
```
#include <sys/stream.h>
#include <sys/ddi.h>

void qenable(queue_t *q);
```

ARGUMENT
q   Pointer to the queue to be enabled.

DESCRIPTION
qenable puts the queue pointed to by *q* on the linked list of those whose service routines are ready to be called by the STREAMS scheduler.

RETURN VALUE
None

LEVEL
Base or Interrupt

SEE ALSO
BCI Driver Development Guide, Chapter 7, "STREAMS"

EXAMPLE
See the dupb(D3DK) function page for an example of the qenable.

qreply (D3DK)

NAME
qreply - send a message on a stream in the reverse direction

SYNOPSIS
```
#include <sys/stream.h>
```
void qreply(queue_t *q, mblk_t *bp);

ARGUMENTS
q   Pointer to the queue.

bp   Pointer to the message to be sent in the opposite direction.

DESCRIPTION
qreply sends a message on a stream in the opposite direction from *q*. It calls the OTHERQ(D3DK) function to find *q*'s module partner, and passes the message by calling the put(D2DK) routine of the next queue in the stream after *q*'s partner.

RETURN VALUE
None

LEVEL
Base or Interrupt

SEE ALSO
BCI Driver Development Guide, Chapter 7, "STREAMS"

STREAMS Programmer's Guide

OTHERQ(D3DK), putnext(D3DK)

EXAMPLE
This example depicts the canonical flushing code for STREAMS drivers. The driver has a write srv(D2DK) (service) routine that may have messages on the queue. If it receives an M_FLUSH message (line 6), and if the FLUSHW bit is on in the first byte of the message (line 7), then the write queue is flushed (line 8) and the FLUSHW bit is turned off (line 9). If the FLUSHR bit is on, then the read queue is flushed (line 12) and the message is sent back up the read side of the stream with the qreply(D3DK) function (line 13). If the FLUSHR bit is off, then the message is freed (line 15). See the example for flushq(D3DK) for the canonical flushing code for modules.

qreply does two things. First, it calls the OTHERQ function to change pointer *q* to the module's other queue(D4DK) structure, reversing the direction of the flow. Then it uses that queue's q_next pointer to call the next module's put(D2DK) routine with the M_IOCNAK message.

```
1   xxxwput(q, mp)
2       queue_t *q;
3       mblk_t *mp;
4   {
5       switch(mp->b_datap->db_type) {
6       case M_FLUSH:
7           if (*mp->b_rptr & FLUSHW) {
8               flushq(q, FLUSHALL);
9               *mp->b_rptr &= ~FLUSHW;
10          }
```

```
11              if (*mp->b_rptr & FLUSHR) {
12                      flushq(RD(q), FLUSHALL);
13                      qreply(q, mp);
14              } else {
15                      freemsg(mp);
16              }
17              break;
        . . .
18      }
19  }
```

NAME

qsize – find the number of messages on a queue

SYNOPSIS

#include <sys/stream.h>

int qsize(queue_t *q);

ARGUMENT

q   Queue to be evaluated.

DESCRIPTION

qsize evaluates the queue *q* and returns the number of messages it contains.

RETURN VALUE

If there are no message on the queue, qsize returns 0. Otherwise, it returns the integer representing the number of messages on the queue.

LEVEL

Base or Interrupt

SEE ALSO

BCI Driver Development Guide, Chapter 7, "STREAMS"

RD (D3DK)

NAME
RD – get pointer to the read queue

SYNOPSIS
```
#include <sys/stream.h>
#include <sys/ddi.h>
```

queue_t RD(queue_t *q);

ARGUMENT
q   Pointer to the *write* queue whose *read* queue is to be returned.

DESCRIPTION
The RD function accepts a *write* queue pointer as an argument and returns a pointer to the *read* queue of the same module.

CAUTION: Make sure the argument to this function is a pointer to a *write* queue. RD will not check for queue type, and a system panic could result if it is not the right type.

RETURN VALUE
The pointer to the *read* queue.

LEVEL
Base or Interrupt

SEE ALSO
BCI Driver Development Guide, Chapter 7, "STREAMS"

WR(D3DK)

EXAMPLE
See the qreply(D3DK) function page for an example of RD.

rmalloc(D3DK)

NAME
rmalloc – allocate space from a private space management map

SYNOPSIS
```
#include <sys/map.h>
#include <sys/ddi.h>
```
unsigned long rmalloc(struct map *mp, long size);

ARGUMENTS
mp Memory map from where the resource is drawn.

size Number of units of the resource.

DESCRIPTION
rmalloc is used by a driver to allocate space from a previously defined and initialized private space management map. The map itself is declared as a structure using the driver prefix in the form *prefix*map. Memory is initially allocated for the map either by a data array, or by the kmem_alloc(D3DK) function. rmalloc is one of five functions used for private map management. The other functions include

    rmfree   Return previously allocated space to a map.
    rminit   Define a map structure and initialize a map table.
    rmwant   Return the number of processes waiting for free space.
    rmsetwant   Increment the count of the number of processes waiting for free space in the map.

The rmalloc function allocates space from a memory map in terms of arbitrary units. The system maintains the map structure by size and index, computed in units appropriate for the memory map. For example, units may be byte addresses, pages of memory, or blocks. The elements of the memory map are sorted by index, and the system uses the *size* member to combine adjacent objects into one memory map entry. The system allocates objects from the memory map on a first-fit basis. The normal return value is an unsigned long set to the value of m_addr from the map structure.

RETURN VALUE
Under normal conditions, rmalloc returns the base of the allocated space. Otherwise, rmalloc function returns a 0 if all memory map entries are already allocated.

LEVEL
Base

Interrupt if rmwant is not set

SEE ALSO
BCI Driver Development Guide, Chapter 6, "Input/Output Operations"

dma_pageio(D3D), rminit(D3DK), rmwant(D3DK), rmfree(D3DK)

EXAMPLE
The following example is a simple memory map, but it illustrates the principles of map management. A driver initializes the map table by calling both the rminit(D3DK) and rmfree(D3DK) functions. rminit(D3DK) establishes the number of slots or entries in the map, and rmfree to initialize the total buffer

rmalloc(D3DK)   **rmalloc(D3DK)**

area the map is to manage. The following example is a fragment from a hypothetical `start` routine and illustrates the following procedures:

> Declaration of the map structure (line 4). The defined map array must be initialized to zero before calling `rminit`.
>
> The use of `kmem_alloc`(D3DK) to allocate memory for the map. This example panics the system if the required amount of memory can not be allocated (lines 10–14).
>
> The use of `mapinit` to configure the total number of entries in the map, and of `rmfree` to configure the total buffer area.

```
1   #define XX_MAPSIZE      12
2   #define XX_BUFSIZE      2560
3
4   struct map  xx_map[XX_MAPSIZE]; /* Space management map for */
5                                   /*    a private buffer      */
    ...
6   xx_start()
7       /*
8        * Allocate private buffer.  If insufficient memory,
9        * display message and halt system.
10       */
11  {
12      register caddr_t bp;

13      if ((bp = kmem_alloc(XX_BUFSIZE, KM_NOSLEEP) == 0) {
14
15          cmn_err(CE_PANIC, "xx_start: kmem_alloc failed before %d buffer
                    allocation", XX_BUFSIZE);
16      } /* endif */
17      /*
18       * Initialize space management map with number
19       * of slots in map.
20       */
21      rminit(xx_map, XX_MAPSIZE);
22      /*
23       * Initialize space management map with total
24       * buffer area it is to manage.
25       */
26      rmfree(xx_map, XX_BUFSIZE, bp);
    ...
```

The `rmalloc`(D3DK) function is then used by the driver's `read` or `write` routine to allocate buffers for specific data transfers. If the appropriate space cannot be allocated, the `rmsetwant`(D3DK) function is used to wait for a free buffer and the process is put to sleep until a buffer is available. When a buffer becomes available, the `rmfree`(D3DK) function is called to return the buffer to the map and to wake the sleeping process (no `wakeup`(D3DK) call is required). The `uiomove`(D3DK) function is used to move the data between user space and local

rmalloc(D3DK)

driver memory. The device then moves data between itself and local driver memory through DMA.

The next example illustrates the following procedures:

The size of the I/O request is calculated and stored in the `size` variable (lines 14–15).

While buffers are available, buffers are allocated through the `rmalloc` function using the `size` value (line 25).

If there are not enough buffers free for use, the `rmsetwant`(D3DK) function is called, and the process is put to sleep (lines 26–28). When a buffer becomes available, the `rmfree`(D3DK) function returns the buffer to the map and wakes the process.

The `uiomove`(D3DK) function is used to move data to the allocated buffer (line 35).

If the address passed to the `uiomove` function is invalid, the `rmfree` function is called to release the previously allocated buffer, and an `EFAULT` error is returned.

```
1   #define XX_MAPPRIO  (PZERO + 6)
2   #define XX_MAPSIZE     12
3   #define XX_BUFSIZE   2560
4   #define XX_MAXSIZE   (XX_BUFSIZE / 4)
5
6   struct map  xx_map[XX_MAPSIZE];       /* Private buffer space map */
7          char xx_buffer[XX_BUFSIZE];    /* driver xx_ buffer area */
...
8   read(dev, uio_p, cred_p)
9       dev_t    dev;
10      uio_t    uio_p;          /* Pointer to uio structure for I/O */
11      cred_t   cred_p;
12
13  register caddr_t addr;
14  register int     size;
15      size = min(COUNT, XX_MAXSIZE);  /* Break large I/O request */
16                                      /* into small ones */
17      /*
18       * Get buffer.  If space is not available, then
19       * request a wakeup when space is returned. Wait
20       * for space; rmfree will check rmsetwant and
21       * supply the wakeup call.
22       */
23      oldlevel = spl4();
24
25      while((addr = (caddr_t)rmalloc(xx_map, size)) == NULL) {
26          rmsetwant(xx_map);
27          sleep(xx_map, XX_MAXPRIO);
28      } /* endwhile */
29      splx(oldlevel);
```

```
30
31      /*
32       * Move data to buffer.  If invalid address is found,
33       * return buffer to map and return error code.
34       */
35      if (uiomove(addr, size, UIO_READ, uio_p) == -1)  {
36          oldlevel = spl4();
37          rmfree(xx_map, size, addr);
38          splx(oldlevel);
39          return(EFAULT);
40      } /* endif */
```

rmfree (D3DK)

NAME
rmfree – free space back into a private space management map

SYNOPSIS
```
#include <sys/map.h>
#include <sys/ddi.h>
```
void rmfree(struct map *mp, long size, unsigned long index);

ARGUMENTS
*mp   Pointer to the map(D4DK) structure.

size   Number of units being freed.

index   Index of the first unit of the allocated resource.

DESCRIPTION
rmfree releases space back into a private space management map. It is the opposite of rmalloc(D3DK), which allocates space that is controlled by a private map structure.

Drivers may define private space management buffers for allocation of memory space, in terms of arbitrary units, using the rmalloc(D3DK), rmfree and rminit(D3DK) functions. The drivers must include the file map.h. The system maintains the memory map list structure by size and index, computed in units appropriate for the memory map. For example, units may be byte addresses, pages of memory, or blocks. The elements of the memory map are sorted by index, and the system uses the size member so that adjacent objects are combined into one memory map entry. The system allocates objects from the memory map on a first-fit basis. rmfree frees up unallocated memory for re-use.

RETURN VALUE
None. However, if the m_addr member of the map structure is returned as 0, the following warning message is displayed on the console:

    WARNING: rmfree map overflow *mp* lost *size* items at *index*

where *mp* is the hexadecimal address of the map structure, *size* is the decimal number of buffers freed, and *index* is the decimal address to the first buffer unit freed.

LEVEL
Base or Interrupt

SEE ALSO
rmalloc(D3DK), rminit(D3DK), rmwant(D3DK)

EXAMPLE
See rmalloc(D3DK).

rminit (D3DK)

NAME
rminit – initialize a private space management map

SYNOPSIS
```
#include <sys/map.h>
#include <sys/ddi.h>
```
void rminit(struct map *`mp`, unsigned long `mapsize`);

ARGUMENTS
`mp`   Pointer to the memory map from where the resource is drawn.

`mapsize`   Number of entries for the memory map table.

DESCRIPTION
The `rminit` function initializes a private map structure that can be used for the allocation of memory space. The map itself is declared as a structure using the driver prefix in the form *prefix*`map`. Memory is initially allocated for the map either by a data array, or by the `kmem_alloc`(D3DK) function.

The driver must initialize the `map` structure by calling `rminit`. However, `rminit` does not cause the memory map entries to be labeled available. This must be done through `rmfree`(D3DK) before objects can actually be allocated from the memory map.

The system maintains the memory map list structure by size and index, computed in units appropriate for the memory map. Units may be byte addresses, pages of memory, or blocks. The elements of the memory map are sorted by index.

Two memory map table entries are reserved for internal system use and they are not available for memory map use.

NOTE: The map array must be initialized to zero before calling `rminit`.

RETURN VALUE
None

LEVEL
Base or Interrupt

SEE ALSO
BCI Driver Development Guide, Chapter 6, "Input/Output Operations"

`rmalloc`(D3DK), `rmwant`(D3DK), `rmfree`(D3DK), `rmsetwant`(D4DK)

EXAMPLE
See `rmalloc`(D3DK).

rmsetwant (D3DK)　　　　　　　　　　　　　　　　　　　　　　　　　　**rmsetwant (D3DK)**

NAME

rmsetwant – set the map's wait flag for a wakeup

SYNOPSIS

#include <sys/map.h> #include <sys/ddi.h>

void rmsetwant(struct map *map_p);

ARGUMENTS

map_p　　Pointer to the map the driver is waiting for.

DESCRIPTION

The rmsetwant function increments the counter on the wait flag of the map pointed to by *map_p*. It is typically called from the driver's read or write routine after an unsuccessful attempt to allocate space from the map using rmalloc(D3DK).

Typically, a driver will sleep on map_p after calling rmsetwant. When the rmfree function returns space to the map, it calls wakeup(D3DK).

RETURN VALUE

None

LEVEL

Base only

SEE ALSO

rmalloc(D3DK), rmfree(D3DK), rminit(D3DK), rmwant(D3DK), map(D4DK)

EXAMPLE

See rmalloc(D3DK).

rmvb (D3DK)

NAME
rmvb – remove a message block from a message

SYNOPSIS
```
#include <sys/stream.h>
```
mblk_t *rmvb(mblk_t *mp, mblk_t *bp);

ARGUMENTS
*mp Message from which a block is to be removed. mblk_t is an instance of the msgb(D4DK) structure.

bp Message block to be removed.

DESCRIPTION
rmvb removes a message block (*bp*) from a message (*mp*), and returns a pointer to the altered message. The message block is not freed, merely removed from the message. It is the module or driver's responsibility to free the message block.

RETURN VALUE
If successful, a pointer to the message (minus the removed block) is returned. The pointer is NULL if *bp* was the only block of the message before rmvb was called. If the designated message block (*bp*) does not exist, −1 is returned.

LEVEL
Base or Interrupt

EXAMPLE
This routine removes all zero-length M_DATA message blocks from the given message. For each message block in the message, save the next message block (line 10). If the current message block is of type M_DATA and has no data in its buffer (line 11), then remove it from the message (line 12) and free it (line 13). In either case, continue with the next message block in the message (line 16).

```
1   void
2   xxclean(mp)
3       mblk_t *mp;
4   {
5       mblk_t *tmp;
6       mblk_t *nmp;
7
8       tmp = mp;
9       while (tmp) {
10          nmp = tmp->b_next;
11          if ((tmp->b_datap->db_type == M_DATA) &&
                (tmp->b_rptr == tmp->b_wptr)) {
12              rmvb(mp, tmp);
13              freeb(tmp);
14          }
15          tmp = nmp;
16      }
17  }
```

rmvq (D3DK)

NAME
rmvq – remove a message from a queue

SYNOPSIS
#include <sys/stream.h>

void rmvq(queue_t *q, mblk_t *mp);

ARGUMENTS
q Queue containing the message to be removed.

mp Message to remove.

DESCRIPTION
rmvq removes a message from a queue. A message can be removed from anywhere on a queue. To prevent modules and drivers from having to deal with the internals of message linkage on a queue, either rmvq or getq(D3DK) should be used to remove a message from a queue.

CAUTION: Make sure that the message *mp* exists to avoid a possible system panic.

RETURN VALUE
None

LEVEL
Base or Interrupt

SEE ALSO
BCI Driver Development Guide, Chapter 7, "STREAMS"

EXAMPLE
This code fragment illustrates how one may flush one type of message from a queue. In this case, only M_PROTO T_DATA_IND messages are flushed. For each message on the queue, if it is an M_PROTO message (line 8) of type T_DATA_IND (line 10), save a pointer to the next message (line 11), remove the T_DATA_IND message (line 12) and free it (line 13). Continue with the next message in the list (line 19).

```
1   mblk_t *mp;
2   mblk_t *nmp;
3   queue_t *q;
4   union T_primitives *tp;
5
6   mp = q->q_first;
7   while (mp) {
8       if (mp->b_datap->db_type == M_PROTO) {
9           tp = (union T_primitives *)mp->b_rptr;
10          if (tp->type == T_DATA_IND) {
11              nmp = mp->b_next;
12              rmvq(q, mp);
13              freemsg(mp);
14              mp = nmp;
15          } else {
16              mp = mp->b_next;
17          }
```

```
18      } else {
19              mp = mp->b_next;
20      }
21 }
```

rmwant (D3DK)   **rmwant (D3DK)**

NAME

rmwant – wait for free memory

SYNOPSIS

```
#include <sys/map.h>
#include <sys/ddi.h>
```

unsigned long rmwant(struct map *map_p);

ARGUMENT

map_p   Pointer to the map(D4DK) structure on which the driver is waiting for space.

DESCRIPTION

The rmwant function returns the number of processes waiting for free space in the map.

RETURN VALUE

The number of processes waiting for free space in the map.

LEVEL

Base or Interrupt

SEE ALSO

BCI Driver Development Guide, Chapter 6, "Input/Output Operations"

rmalloc(D3DK), rminit(D3DK), rmfree(D3DK), rmsetwant(D3DK), map(D4DK)

SAMESTR (D3DK)

NAME
SAMESTR – test if next queue is same type

SYNOPSIS
#include <sys/stream.h>

int SAMESTR(queue_t *q);

ARGUMENT
*q   Pointer to the queue.

DESCRIPTION
The SAMESTR function is used to see if the next queue in a stream (if it exists) is the same type as the current queue (that is, both are read queues or both are write queues).

RETURN VALUE
SAMESTR returns 1 if the next queue is the same type as the current queue. It returns 0 if the next queue does not exist or if it is not the same type.

LEVEL
Base or Interrupt

SEE ALSO
OTHERQ(D3DK)

sleep (D3DK)   sleep (D3DK)

NAME
    sleep – suspend process activity pending execution of an event

SYNOPSIS
    #include <sys/types.h>
    #include <sys/param.h>

    int sleep(caddr_t *event*, int *priority*);

ARGUMENTS
    event   Address (signifying an event) for which the process will wait to be updated.

    priority   Priority that is assigned to the process when it is awakened. If *priority* is ORed with the defined constant PCATCH, the sleep function does not call longjmp on receipt of a signal. Instead, it returns the value 1 to the calling routine.

DESCRIPTION
    sleep suspends execution of a process to await certain events such as reaching a known system state in hardware or software. For instance, when a process wants to read a device and no data is available, the driver may need to call sleep to wait for data to become available before returning. This causes the kernel to suspend executing the process that called sleep and schedule another process. The process that called sleep can be restarted by a call to the wakeup(D3DK) function with the same *event* specified as that used to call sleep.

    A driver (with data stored in local variables) may call sleep while waiting for an event to occur. Make sure another process will not interrupt the driver and overwrite the local variables.

    The *event* address used when calling sleep should be the address of a kernel data structure or one of the driver's own data structures. The sleep address is an arbitrary address that has no meaning except to the corresponding wakeup function call. This does not mean that any arbitrary kernel address should be used for sleep. Doing this could conflict with other, unrelated sleep/wakeup operations in the kernel. A kernel address used for sleep should be the address of a kernel data structure directly associated with the driver I/O operation (for example, a buffer assigned to the driver).

    Before a process calls sleep, the driver usually sets a flag in a driver data structure indicating the reason why sleep is being called.

    The *priority* argument, called the sleep priority, is used for scheduling purposes when the process awakens. This parameter has critical effects on how the process that called sleep reacts to signals. If the numerical value of the sleep priority is less than or equal to the constant PZERO (defined in the sys/param.h header file), then the sleeping process will not be awakened by a signal. However, if the numerical value is greater than PZERO, the system awakens the process that called sleep prematurely (that is, before the event on which sleep was called occurred) on receipt of a non-ignored, non-held signal. In this case, it returns the value 1 to the calling routine if PCATCH is set; otherwise it does a longjmp and never returns to the driver. If the event occurred, 0 is returned.

sleep (D3DK)

To pick the correct `sleep` priority, base your decision on whether or not the process should be awakened on the receipt of a signal. If the driver calls `sleep` for an event that is certain to happen, the driver should use a priority numerically less than or equal to `PZERO`. (However, you should only use priorities less than or equal to `PZERO` if your driver is crucial to system operation.) If the driver calls `sleep` while it awaits an event that may not happen, use a priority numerically greater than `PZERO`.

An example of an event that may not happen is the arrival of data from a remote device. When the system tries to read data from a terminal, the terminal driver might call `sleep` to suspend the current process while waiting for data to arrive from the terminal. If data never arrives, the `sleep` call will never be answered. When a user at the terminal presses the BREAK key or hangs up, the terminal driver interrupt handler sends a signal to the reading process, which is still executing `sleep`. The signal causes the reading process to finish the system call without having read any data. If `sleep` is called with a priority value that is not awakened by signals, the process can be awakened only by a specific `wakeup` call. If that `wakeup` call never happened (the user hung up the terminal), then the process executes `sleep` until the system is rebooted.

Another important criteria for selecting the appropriate priority is how important the event or resource being waited for is to overall system performance. For example, disk I/O is often a bottleneck, so the priority for disk I/O is higher than most other priorities. In contrast, terminal I/O is a much lower priority. The sooner the process runs, the faster the resource will be used and freed again.

Drivers calling `sleep` must occasionally perform cleanup operations before returning. Typical items that need cleaning up are locked data structures that should be unlocked when the system call completes. This is done by ORing *priority* with `PCATCH` and executing `sleep`. If `sleep` returns a 1, then you can cleanup any locked structures or free any allocated resources, and return. CAUTION: If `sleep` is called from the driver `strategy(D2DK)` routine, you should OR the *priority* argument with `PCATCH` or select a *priority* of `PZERO` or less.

RETURN VALUE

If the `sleep` *priority* argument is ORed with the defined constant `PCATCH`, the `sleep` function does not call `longjmp` on receipt of a signal; instead, it returns the value 1 to the calling routine. If the process put in a wait state by `sleep` is awakened by an explicit `wakeup` call rather than by a signal, the `sleep` call returns 0.

LEVEL

Base Only (Do not call from an interrupt routine)

SEE ALSO

BCI Driver Development Guide, Chapter 10, "Synchronizing Hardware and Software Events"

delay(D3DK), biodone(D3DK), biowait(D3DK), timeout(D3DK), untimeout(D3DK), wakeup(D3DK)

sleep (D3DK)   **sleep (D3DK)**

EXAMPLE

See the untimeout(D3DK) function page for an example of `sleep`.

spl(D3D)

NAME
spl – block/allow interrupts

SYNOPSIS
```
#include <sys/inline.h>

int spl0();
int spl1();
int spl4();
int spl5();
int spl6();
int spl7();
int splvm();
int splhi();
int splstr();
int spltty();

int splx(int oldlevel);
```

ARGUMENT
oldlevel   Last set priority value (only `splx` has an input argument).

DESCRIPTION
`spl` blocks or allows interrupts. When a process is executing code in a driver, the system will not switch context from that process to another executing process unless it is explicitly told to do so by the driver. This protects the integrity of the kernel and driver data structures. However, the system does allow devices to interrupt the processor and handle these interrupts immediately.

The integrity of system data structures would be destroyed if an interrupt handler were to manipulate the same data structures as a process executing in the driver. To prevent such problems, the kernel provides the `spl` functions allowing a driver to set processor execution levels, prohibiting the handling of interrupts below the level set.

The selection of the appropriate `spl` function is important. The execution level to which the processor is set must be high enough to protect the region of code; but this level should not be so high that it unnecessarily locks out interrupts that need to be processed quickly. A hardware device is assigned to an interrupt priority level depending on the type of device. By using the appropriate `spl` function, a driver can inhibit interrupts from its device or other devices at the same or lower interrupt priority levels.

The `spl` command changes the state of the processor status word (PSW). The PSW stores the current processor execution level, in addition to information relating to the operating system internals. The `spl` functions block out interrupts that come in at a priority level at or below a machine-dependent interrupt priority level. The `spl` functions include the following:

   spl0   Restores all interrupts when executing on the base level. A driver routine may use `spl0` when the routine has been called through a system call; that is, if it is known that the level being restored is indeed at base level.

spl(D3D)   **spl(D3D)**

spl1	Used in context and process switch to protect critical code.
spl4	Used in character drivers to protect critical code.
spl5	Used in character drivers to protect critical code (this function has the same effect as spl4).
spl6	Used in block drivers to protect critical code.
spl7	Used in any type of driver to mask out all interrupts including the clock, and should be used very sparingly.
splvm	Used in memory management code to protect critical regions.
splhi	Used in any type of driver to mask out all interrupts including the clock, and should be used very sparingly. (This function is identical to spl7.)
spltty	Used by a TTY driver to protect critical code.
splstr	Used to protect STREAMS driver and module critical regions of code. This is defined to be high enough to block interrupts from the highest priority STREAMS device. splstr is mapped to spltty.
splx	Used to terminate a section of protected critical code. This function restores the interrupt level to the previous level specified by its argument *oldlevel*.

NOTE: spl functions should not be used in interrupt routines unless you save the old interrupt priority level in a variable as it was returned from an spl call. Later, splx must be used to restore the saved old level. Never drop the interrupt priority level below the level at which an interrupt routine was entered. For example, if an interrupt routine is entered at the interrupt priority level of an spl6, do not call spl0 through spl5 or the stack may become corrupted.

RETURN VALUE

All spl functions (except splx) return the former priority level.

EXAMPLE

See the untimeout(D3DK) function page for an example of spl.

strlog (D3DK)

NAME
strlog – submit messages to the `log` driver

SYNOPSIS
```
#include <sys/stream.h>
#include <sys/strlog.h>
#include <sys/log.h>
```
int strlog(short *mid*, short *sid*, char *level*, unsigned short *flags*,
    char *fmt, unsigned *arg1*, ...);

ARGUMENTS
mid   Identification number of the module or driver submitting the message.

sid   Identification number for a particular minor device.

level   Tracing level for selective screening of low priority messages.

flags   Valid flag values are:

SL_ERROR	Message is for error logger.
SL_TRACE	Message is for trace.
SL_NOTIFY	Mail copy of message to system administrator.
SL_CONSOLE	Log message to console.
SL_FATAL	Error is fatal.
SL_WARN	Error is a warning.
SL_NOTE	Error is a notice.

fmt   printf(3S) style format string. %s, %e, %g, and %G formats are not allowed.

arg1   Zero or more arguments to printf.

DESCRIPTION
strlog submits formatted messages to the log(7) driver. The messages can be retrieved with the getmsg(2) system call. The *flags* argument specifies the type of the message and where it is to be sent. strace(1M) receives messages from the log driver and sends them to the standard output. strerr(1M) receives error messages from the log driver and appends them to a file called /var/adm/streams/error.*mm-dd*, where *mm-dd* identifies the date of the error message.

RETURN VALUE
strlog returns 0 if the message is not seen by all the readers, 1 otherwise.

LEVEL
Base or Interrupt

SEE ALSO
BCI Driver Development Guide, Chapter 12, "Error Reporting"

log(7)

strqget (D3DK)

NAME
strqget – get information about a queue or band of the queue

SYNOPSIS
```
#include <sys/stream.h>

int strqget(queue_t *q, qfields_t what, unsigned char pri,
    long *valp);
```

ARGUMENTS
q   Pointer to the queue

what   Which field of the `queue` structure to return information about. Valid values are specified in `stream.h`:

```
typedef enum qfields {
        QHIWAT   = 0,    /* q_hiwat or qb_hiwat */
        QLOWAT   = 1,    /* q_lowat or qb_lowat */
        QMAXPSZ  = 2,    /* q_maxpsz */
        QMINPSZ  = 3,    /* q_minpsz */
        QCOUNT   = 4,    /* q_count or qb_count */
        QFIRST   = 5,    /* q_first or qb_first */
        QLAST    = 6,    /* q_last or qb_last */
        QFLAG    = 7,    /* q_flag or qb_flag */
        QBAD     = 8
} qfields_t;
```

pri   Priority of request.

valp   The value for the requested field.

DESCRIPTION
`strqget` gives drivers and modules a way to get information about a queue or a particular band of a queue without directly accessing STREAMS data structures.

RETURN VALUE
On success, 0 is returned. An error number is returned on failure.

LEVEL
Base or Interrupt

SEE ALSO
BCI Driver Development Guide, Chapter 7, "STREAMS"

strqset(D3DK)

strqset(D3DK) strqset(D3DK)

NAME
strqset – change information about a queue or band of the queue

SYNOPSIS
#include <sys/stream.h>

int strqset(queue_t *q, qfields_t *what*, unsigned char *pri*,
    long **val*);

ARGUMENTS
q Pointer to the queue.

what Which field of the `queue` structure to return information about. Valid values are specified in `stream.h`:

```
typedef enum qfields {
    QHIWAT   = 0,    /* q_hiwat or qb_hiwat */
    QLOWAT   = 1,    /* q_lowat or qb_lowat */
    QMAXPSZ  = 2,    /* q_maxpsz */
    QMINPSZ  = 3,    /* q_minpsz */
    QCOUNT   = 4,    /* q_count or qb_count */
    QFIRST   = 5,    /* q_first or qb_first */
    QLAST    = 6,    /* q_last or qb_last */
    QFLAG    = 7,    /* q_flag or qb_flag */
    QBAD     = 8
} qfields_t;
```

pri Priority of request.

val The value for the field to be changed.

DESCRIPTION
`strqset` gives drivers and modules a way to change information about a queue or a particular band of a queue without directly accessing STREAMS data structures. The fields that can be returned are defined in the enumerated type `qfields`. `qfields` defines the following fields:

RETURN VALUE
On success, 0 is returned. An error number is returned on failure. If the *what* field is read-only, `EPERM` is returned and the field is left unchanged.

LEVEL
Base or Interrupt

SEE ALSO
BCI Driver Development Guide, Chapter 7, "STREAMS"

strqget(D3DK)

testb (D3DK)

NAME
testb – check for an available buffer

SYNOPSIS
```
#include <sys/stream.h>

int testb(int size, int pri);
```

ARGUMENTS
size   Size of the requested buffer.

pri   Priority of the allocb request.

DESCRIPTION
testb checks to see if an allocb(D3DK) call is likely to succeed if a buffer of *size* bytes at priority *pri* is requested. Even if testb returns successfully, the call to allocb can fail.

RETURN VALUE
Returns 1 if a buffer of the requested size is available, and 0 if one is not.

LEVEL
Base or Interrupt

SEE ALSO
BCI Driver Development Guide, Chapter 7, "STREAMS"

allocb(D3DK), bufcall(D3DK)

EXAMPLE
In a srv(D2DK) (service) routine, if copymsg(D3DK) fails (line 6), the message is put back on the queue (line 7) and a routine, tryagain, is scheduled to be run in one tenth of a second (HZ/10). Then the service routine returns.

When the timeout(D3DK) function runs, if there is no message on the front of the queue, it just returns. Otherwise, for each message block in the first message, check to see if an allocation would succeed. If the number of message blocks equals the number we can allocate, then enable the service procedure. Otherwise, reschedule tryagain to run again in another tenth of a second. Note that tryagain is merely an approximation. Its accounting may be faulty. Consider the case of a message comprised of two 1024-byte message blocks. If there is only one free 1024-byte message block and no free 2048-byte message blocks, then testb will still succeed twice. If no message blocks are freed of these sizes before the service procedure runs again, then the copymsg(D3DK) will still fail. The reason testb is used here is because it is significantly faster than calling copymsg. We must minimize the amount of time spent in a timeout routine.

```
1   xxxsrv(q)
2       queue_t *q;
3   {
4       mblk_t *mp;
5       mblk_t *nmp;
         . . .
6       if ((nmp = copymsg(mp)) == NULL) {
7           putbq(q, mp);
8           timeout(tryagain, (long)q, HZ/10);
```

```
 9              return;
10      }
        . . .
11  }
12
13  tryagain(q)
14      queue_t *q;
15  {
16      register int can_alloc = 0;
17      register int num_blks = 0;
18      register mblk_t *mp;
19
20      if (!q->q_first)
21              return;
22      for (mp = q->q_first; mp; mp = mp->b_cont) {
23              num_blks++;
24              can_alloc += testb((mp->b_datap->db_lim -
25                  mp->b_datap->db_base), BPRI_MED);
26      }
27      if (num_blks == can_alloc)
28              qenable(q);
29      else
30              timeout(tryagain, (long)q, HZ/10);
31  }
```

timeout (D3DK)

NAME
timeout – execute a function after a specified length of time

SYNOPSIS
```
#include <sys/types.h>

int timeout(int (*ftn)(), caddr_t arg, long ticks);
```

ARGUMENTS
ftn   Kernel function to invoke when the time increment expires.

arg   Argument to the function.

ticks   Number of clock ticks to wait before the function is called.

DESCRIPTION
The timeout function schedules the specified function to be called after a specified time interval. Control is immediately returned to the caller. This is useful when an event is known to occur within a specific time frame, or when you want to wait for I/O processes when an interrupt is not available or might cause problems. For example, some robotics applications do not provide a status flag for determining when to pump information to the robot's controller. By using timeout, the driver can wait a predetermined interval and then begin transferring data to the robot.

The exact time interval over which the timeout takes effect cannot be guaranteed, but the value given is a close approximation. The function called by timeout must adhere to the same restrictions as a driver interrupt handler. It can neither sleep nor use previously set local variables.

RETURN VALUE
Under normal conditions, an integer timeout identifier is returned (which may, in unusual circumstances, be set to 0). Otherwise, if the timeout table is full, the following panic message results:

    PANIC: Timeout table overflow

The timeout function returns an identifier that may be passed to the untimeout(D3DK) function to cancel a pending request. **NOTE:** No value is returned from the called function.

LEVEL
Base or Interrupt

SEE ALSO
BCI Driver Development Guide, Chapter 10, "Synchronizing Hardware and Software Events"

delay(D3DKK), biodone(D3DK), biowait(D3DK), sleep(D3DK), untimeout(D3DK), wakeup(D3DK)

EXAMPLE
See the bufcall(D3DK) function page for an example of timeout.

NAME

uiomove – copy kernel data using uio(D4DK) structure

SYNOPSIS

```
#include <sys/types.h>
#include <sys/uio.h>

int uiomove(caddr_t address, long nbytes, enum uio_rw rwflag,
    struct uio * uio_p);
```

ARGUMENTS

address   Source/destination kernel address of the copy.

nbytes   Number of bytes to copy.

rwflag   Flag indicating read or write operation. Possible values are UIO_READ and UIO_WRITE.

uio_p   Pointer to the uio structure for the copy.

DESCRIPTION

The uiomove function copies *nbytes* of data to or from the space defined by the uio structure (described in uio.h) and the driver.

The uio_segflg member of the uio structure determines the the type of space to or from which the transfer being made. If it is set to UIO_SYSSPACE the data transfer is between addresses in the kernel. If it is set to UIO_USERSPACE the transfer is between a user program and kernel space.

In addition to moving the data, uiomove adds the number of bytes moved to the iov_base member of the iovec(D4DK) structure, decreases the iov_len member, increases the uio_offset member of the uio structure, and decreases the uio_resid member.

This function does automatic page boundary checking. *nbytes* does not have to be word-aligned.

CAUTION: If uio_segflg is set to UIO_SYSSPACE and *address* is selected from user space, the system panics.

RETURN VALUE

uiomove returns 0 upon success or −1 on failure. The driver entry point routine through which uiomove was called should return EFAULT if −1 is returned.

LEVEL

Base.

SEE ALSO

uio(D4DK), ureadc(D3DK), uwritec(D3DK)

EXAMPLE

See rmalloc.

NAME
unlinkb – remove a message block from the head of a message

SYNOPSIS
```
#include <sys/stream.h>
```
mblk_t *unlinkb(mblk_t *mp);

ARGUMENT
mp   Pointer to the message.

DESCRIPTION
unlinkb removes the first message block from the message pointed to by *mp*. A new message, minus the removed message block, is returned.

RETURN VALUE
If successful, unlinkb returns a pointer to the message with the first message block removed. If there is only one message block in the message, NULL is returned.

LEVEL
Base or Interrupt

SEE ALSO
BCI Driver Development Guide, Chapter 7, "STREAMS"

linkb(D3DK)

EXAMPLE
The routine expects to get passed an M_PROTO T_DATA_IND message. It will remove and free the M_PROTO header and return the remaining M_DATA portion of the message.

```
1   mblk_t *
2   makedata(mp)
3       mblk_t *mp;
4   {
5       mblk_t *nmp;
6
7       nmp = unlinkb(mp);
8       freeb(mp);
9       return(nmp);
10  }
```

untimeout (D3DK)   untimeout (D3DK)

NAME
untimeout – cancel previous timeout(D3DK) function call
SYNOPSIS
    #include <sys/types.h>

    int untimeout(int *id*);
ARGUMENTS
id   Identification value generated by a previous timeout function call.
DESCRIPTION
untimeout cancels a pending timeout(D3DK) request.
RETURN VALUE
None
LEVEL
Base or Interrupt
SEE ALSO
BCI Driver Development Guide, Chapter 10, "Synchronizing Hardware and Software Events"

delay(D3DK), biodone(D3DK), biowait(D3DK), sleep(D3DK), timeout(D3DK), wakeup(D3DK)
EXAMPLE
A driver may have to repeatedly request outside help from a computer operator. The timeout function is used to delay a certain amount of time between requests. However, once the request is honored, the driver will want to cancel the timeout operation. This is done with the untimeout function.

In a driver open(D2DK) routine, after the input arguments have been verified, the status of the device is tested. If the device is not on-line, a message is displayed on the system console. The driver schedules a wakeup(D3DK) call and waits for five minutes (line 41). If the device is still not ready, the procedure is repeated.

When the device is made ready, an interrupt is generated. The driver interrupt handling routine notes there is a suspended process. It cancels the timeout request (line 59) and wakens the suspended process (line 61).

```
1   struct  mtu_device  {
2                              /* layout of physical device registers */
3           int     control;   /* physical device control word        */
4           int     status;    /* physical device status word         */
5           int     byte_cnt;  /* number of bytes to be transferred   */
6           paddr_t baddr:     /* DMA starting physical address       */
7   }; /* end device */
8
9   struct mtu      {
10                             /* magnetic tape unit logical structure */
11          struct buf *mtu_head;  /* pointer to I/O queue head        */
12          struct buf *mtu_tail;  /* pointer to buffer I/O queue tail */
13          int        mtu_flag;   /* logical status flag              */
```

untimeout (D3DK)

```
14          int         mtu_to_id; /* time out ID number              */
            ...
15  }; /* end mtu */
16
17  extern struct mtu_device *mtu_addr[];     /* location of dev regs */
18  extern struct mtu         mtu_tbl[];      /* location of dev structs */
19  extern int     mtu_cnt;
      ...
20  mtu_open(dev, flag, type, c_ptr)
21      dev_t dev;
22  {
23      register struct mtu *dp;
24      register struct mtu_device *rp;
25      if ((getminor(dev) >> 3) > mtu_cnt) { /* if dev doesn't exist */
26          return(ENXIO);               /* then return error condition */
27      } /* endif */
28
29      dp = &mtu_tbl[getminor(dev)];    /* get logical device struct */
30      if  (dp->mtu_flag & MTU_BUSY) != 0) { /* if device is in use, */
31          return(EBUSY);                    /* return busy status */
32      } /* endif */
33
34      dp->mtu_flag = MTU_BUSY;  /* mark device in use & clear flags */
35      rp = xx_addr[getminor(dev) >> 3];          /* get device regs */
36      oldlevel2 = splhi();
37      while((rp->status & MTU_LOAD) == 0) { /* while tape not loaded */
38                              /* display mount request on console */
39          cmn_err(CE_NOTE, "!Tape MOUNT, drive %d", minor(dev) & 0x3);
40          dp->mtu_flag |= MTU_WAIT;  /* indicate process suspended */
41          dp->mtu_to_id = timeout(wakeup, dp, 5*60*HZ); /* wait 5 min */
42          if (sleep(dp, (PCATCH | PZERO+2)) == 1){/*wait on tape load */
43                              /* if user aborts process, release */
44              dp->mtu_flag = 0;    /* tape device by clearing flags */
45              untimeout(dp->mtu_to_id);
46              splx(oldlevel2);
47          } /* endif */
48      } /* endwhile */
49      splx(oldlevel2);
50  } /* end mtu_open */
      ...
51  mtu_int(cntr)
52      int cntr;            /* controller that caused the interrupt */
53  {
54  register struct mtu_device *rp = xx_addr[cntr]; /* get device regs */
55  register struct mtu *dp = &mtu_tbl[cntr << 3 | (rp->status & 0x3)];
      ...
56      if ((dp->mtu_flag & MTU_WAIT) != 0){ /* if process is suspended */
57                                     /* waiting for tape mount, */
58          untimeout(dp->mtu_to_id);       /* cancel timeout request */
```

```
59          dp->flag &= ~MTU_WAIT;           /* clear wait flag */
60          wakeup(dp);                      /* awaken suspended process */
61      } /* endif */
        ...
```

NAME

ureadc – add character to a uio structure

SYNOPSIS

#include <sys/uio.h>

int ureadc(int *c*, uio_t **uio_p*);

ARGUMENTS

c　　　　The character added to the uio structure.

*uio_p　　Pointer to the uio(D4DK) structure.

DESCRIPTION

ureadc transfers the character *c* into the address space of the uio structure pointed to by *uio_p*, and updates the uio structure as for uiomove(D3DK).

RETURN VALUE

0 is returned on success and EFAULT on failure.

LEVEL

Base or Interrupt

SEE ALSO

uiomove(D3DK), uwritec(D3DK), iovec(D4DK), uio(D4DK)

useracc(D3DK) useracc(D3DK)

NAME
useracc – verify whether user has access to memory

SYNOPSIS
```
#include <sys/types.h>
#include <sys/buf.h>
```
int useracc(caddr_t *base*, uint *count*, int *access*);

ARGUMENTS
base The start address of the user data area

count The size of the data transfer in bytes

access A flag to determine whether the access is a read or write. The defined constant B_READ specifies a read from the device and a write to memory. This requires that the user have write access permission for the specified data area. The defined constant B_WRITE specifies a read from memory and a write to the device. It requires read access permission for the data area. (B_READ and B_WRITE are defined in the system header file sys/buf.h.)

DESCRIPTION
useracc verifies if a user has proper access to memory. It is not necessary to use useracc for buffered I/O (including use of the copyin(D3DK) and copyout(D3DK) functions).

RETURN VALUE
Under normal conditions, 1 is returned. If the user does not have the proper access permission to the memory specified return EFAULT.

LEVEL
Base Only (Do not call from an interrupt routine)

SEE ALSO
drv_priv(D3DK)

uwritec(D3DK)

NAME

uwritec – remove a character from a uio structure

SYNOPSIS

```
#include <sys/uio.h>
```

int uwritec (uio_t *uio_p);

ARGUMENTS

uio_p   Pointer to the uio(D4DK) structure.

DESCRIPTION

uwritec returns a character from the uio structure pointed to by *uio_p*, and updates the uio structure as for uiomove(D3DK).

RETURN VALUE

The next character for processing is returned on success, and −1 is returned if uio is empty or there is an error.

LEVEL

Base or Interrupt

SEE ALSO

uiomove(D3DK), ureadc(D3DK), iovec(D4DK), uio(D4DK)

vtop (D3D)   **vtop (D3D)**

NAME
　　vtop – convert virtual to physical address

SYNOPSIS
　　#include <sys/types.h>

　　paddr_t vtop(long *vaddr*, proc_t **p*);

ARGUMENTS
　　vaddr　　　Virtual address to convert.

　　p　　　　　Pointer to the proc(D4X) structure used by vtop to locate the information tables used for memory management. To indicate that the address is in kernel virtual space or in the virtual space of the current process, set *p* to NULL. Block drivers that can transfer data directly in and out of user memory space must set *p* to the b_proc member of the buf(D4DK) structure.

DESCRIPTION
　　vtop converts a virtual address to a physical address. When a driver receives a memory address from the kernel, that address is virtual. Generally, memory management is performed by the MMU. However, devices that access memory directly (DMA) deal only with physical memory addresses. In such cases, the driver must provide the device with physical memory addresses.

　　The virtual address is the memory address being translated. The vtop function returns the translated address.

　　The same functionality is provided by the kvtophys(D3D) function.

RETURN VALUE
　　Under normal conditions, a physical address is returned. Otherwise, the following can be returned:

　　　　–1　if the virtual address to be translated is not a valid one

　　　　 0　if there is no physical memory mapped to the virtual address

LEVEL
　　Base or Interrupt.

SEE ALSO
　　BCI Driver Development Guide, Chapter 6, "Input/Output Operations"

　　btop(D3DK), btopr(D3DK), ptob(D3DK), kvtophys(D3D)

wakeup (D3DK)   **wakeup (D3DK)**

NAME
wakeup – resume suspended process execution

SYNOPSIS
```
#include <sys/types.h>

void wakeup(caddr_t event);
```

ARGUMENT
event   Address that is the same address used by sleep(D3DK) to suspend process execution.

DESCRIPTION
wakeup awakens all processes that called sleep with an address as the *event* argument. This lets the processes execute according to the scheduler. Ensure that the same *event* argument is used for both sleep and wakeup. It is recommended for code readability and for efficiency to have a one-to-one correspondence between events and sleep addresses. Also, there is usually one bit in the driver flag member that corresponds to the reason for calling sleep.

Whenever a driver calls sleep, it should test to ensure the event on which the driver called sleep occurred. There is an interval between the time the process that called sleep is awakened and the time it resumes execution where the state forcing the sleep may have been reentered. This can occur because all processes waiting for an event are awakened at the same time. The first process given control by the scheduler usually gains control of the event. All other processes awakened should recognize that they cannot continue and should reissue sleep.

RETURN VALUE
None

LEVEL
Base or Interrupt

SEE ALSO
BCI Driver Development Guide, Chapter 10, "Synchronizing Hardware and Software Events"

delay(D3DK), biodone(D3DK), biowait(D3DK), sleep(D3DK), timeout(D3DK), untimeout(D3DK)

EXAMPLE
See the untimeout(D3DK) function page for an example of wakeup.

WR (D3DK)

NAME
WR − get pointer to the write queue for this module or driver

SYNOPSIS
```
#include <sys/stream.h>
#include <sys/ddi.h>

queue_t WR(queue_t *q);
```

ARGUMENTS
q   Pointer to the *read* queue whose *write* queue is to be returned.

DESCRIPTION
The **WR** function accepts a *read* queue pointer as an argument and returns a pointer to the *write* queue of the same module.

CAUTION: Make sure the argument to this function is a pointer to a *read* queue. WR will not check for queue type, and a system panic could result if the pointer is not to a *read* queue.

RETURN VALUE
The pointer to the *write* queue.

LEVEL
Base or Interrupt

SEE ALSO
STREAMS Programmer's Guide

OTHERQ(D3DK), RD(D3DK)

EXAMPLE
In a STREAMS `close` routine, the driver or module is passed a pointer to the read queue. The driver must zero out the `q_ptr` field of both the read and write queues if it had previously initialized them in its `open` routine. These usually are set to the address of the module-specific data structure for the minor device.

```
1   xxxclose(q, flag)
2       queue_t *q;
3       int flag;
4   {
5       q->q_ptr = NULL;
6       WR(q)->q_ptr = NULL;
        . . .
7   }
```

4. DATA STRUCTURE (D4)

4. DATA STRUCTURE (D4)

4 Data Structures (D4)

Introduction	4-1

Manual Pages	4-3
buf(D4DK)	4-3
cred(D4DK)	4-7
datab(D4DK)	4-8
free_rtn(D4DK)	4-9
hdedata(D4D)	4-10
iovec(D4DK)	4-11
map(D4DK)	4-12
module_info(D4DK)	4-13
msgb(D4DK)	4-14
qband(D4DK)	4-15
qinit(D4DK)	4-16
queue(D4DK)	4-17
streamtab(D4DK)	4-18
uio(D4DK)	4-19

Introduction

This chapter describes the data structures used by drivers to share information between the driver and the kernel. All driver data structures shared by both DDI and DKI are identified with the (D4DK) cross reference code. All DDI-only or DKI-only structures are identified with the (D4D) or (D4K) cross reference codes respectively.

In this section, reference pages contain the following headings:

- NAME summarizes the structure's purpose.
- SYNOPSIS lists the include file that defines the structure.
- DESCRIPTION provides general information about the structure.
- STRUCTURE MEMBERS lists all accessible structure members.
- SEE ALSO gives sources for further information.

Table 4-1 summarizes the STREAMS structures described in this section. STREAMS structures may be used in either DDI or DKI.

Table 4-1: STREAMS Data Structure Summary

Routine	Description
datab	STREAMS message data structure
free_rtn	structure specifying routine that frees non-STREAMS data buffers
module_info	STREAMS driver identification and limit value structure
msgb	STREAMS message block structure
qband	STREAMS queue flow control information structure
qinit	structure specifying STREAMS queue processing procedures
queue	STREAMS queue structure
streamtab	structure specifying qinit structures

Introduction

Table 4-2 summarizes structures that are not specific to STREAMS I/O. These structures may be used in either DDI or DKI, except as noted.

Table 4-2: Data Structures not Specific to STREAMS

Routine	Description	Type
buf	block I/O data transfer structure	
cred	access credential structure	
hdedata	hard disk error data structure	DDI only
iovec	structure specifying address and size of I/O request using uio(D4DK)	
map	private memory map structure	
uio	scatter/gather I/O request structure	

 Do not declare arrays of structures as the size of the structures may change between releases. Rely only on the structure members listed in this chapter and not on unlisted members or the position of a member in a structure.

buf(D4DK)

NAME
buf – block I/O data transfer structure

SYNOPSIS
`#include <sys/buf.h>`

DESCRIPTION
The `buf` structure is the basic data structure for block I/O transfers. Each block I/O transfer has an associated buffer header. The header contains all the buffer control and status information. For drivers, the buffer header pointer is the sole argument to a block driver **strategy**(D2DK) routine. Do not depend on the size of the `buf` structure when writing a driver.

It is important to note that a buffer header may be linked in multiple lists simultaneously. Because of this, most of the members in the buffer header cannot be changed by the driver, even when the buffer header is in one of the drivers' work lists.

Buffer headers are also used by the system for unbuffered or physical I/O for block drivers. In this case, the buffer describes a portion of user data space that is locked into memory (see **physiock**(D3D)).

Block drivers often chain block requests so that overall throughput for the device is maximized. The `av_forw` and the `av_back` members of the `buf` structure can serve as link pointers for chaining block requests.

The following figure illustrates two linked lists of buffers. The top illustration is the `bfreelist`, the list of available buffers. The bottom illustration is a queue of allocated buffers. The lined areas indicate other buffer members.

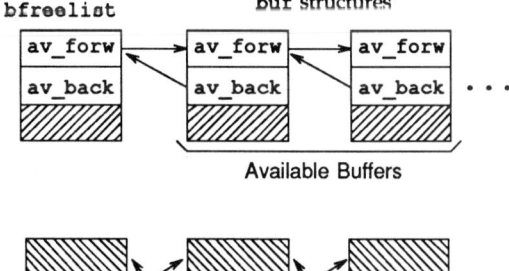

STRUCTURE MEMBERS

buf(D4DK) buf(D4DK)

```
int            b_flags;       /* Buffer status */
struct buf     *b_forw;       /* headed by d_tab of conf.c */
struct buf     *b_back;       /* headed by d_tab of conf.c */
struct buf     *av_forw;      /* Driver work list link */
struct buf     *av_back;      /* Driver work lists link */
o_dev_t        b_dev;         /* Major/minor device numbers */
unsigned       b_bcount;      /* # of bytes to transfer */
caddr_t        b_addr;        /* Buffer's virtual address */
daddr_t        b_blkno;       /* Block number on device */
char           b_oerror;      /* Old post-I/O error number */
unsigned int   b_resid;       /* # of bytes not transferred */
clock_t        b_start;       /* request start time */
struct proc    *b_proc;       /* Process table entry address */
struct page    *b_pages;      /* page list for PAGEIO */
unsigned long  b_reltime;     /* previous release time */
long           b_bufsize;     /* size of allocated buffer */
int            (*b_iodone);   /* function called by biodone */
struct vnode   *b_vp;         /* vnode associated with block */
int            b_error;       /* expanded error field */
dev_t          b_edev;        /* expanded dev field */
```

CAUTION: Buffers are a shared resource within the kernel. Drivers should read or write only the members listed in this section. Drivers that attempt to use undocumented members of the buf structure risk corrupting data in the kernel or on the device.

The paddr macro (defined in buf.h) provides access to the b_un.b_addr member of the buf structure. (b_un is a union that contains b_addr.)

The members of the buffer header available to test or set by a driver are as follows:

b_flags stores the buffer status and tells the driver whether to read or write to the device. The driver must never clear the b_flags member. If this is done, unpredictable results can occur including loss of disk sanity and the possible failure of other kernel processes.

Valid flags are as follows:

B_BUSY   indicates the buffer is in use.

B_DONE   indicates the data transfer has completed.

B_ERROR   indicates an I/O transfer error.

B_KERNBUF   indicates the buffer is allocated by the kernel and not by a driver.

B_PAGEIO   indicates the buffer is being used in a paged I/O request. If B_PAGEIO is set, the b_pages field of the buffer header will point to a sorted list of page structures. Also, the b_addr field of the buffer header will be offset into the first page of the page list. If B_PAGEIO is not set, the b_addr field of the buffer header will contain the kernel virtual address of the I/O request. The b_pages field of

buf(D4DK)

the buffer header is not used.

B_PHYS indicates the buffer header is being used for physical (direct) I/O to a user data area. The b_un member contains the starting address of the user data area.

B_READ indicates data is to be read from the peripheral device into main memory.

B_WANTED indicates the buffer is sought for allocation.

B_WRITE indicates the data is to be transferred from main memory to the peripheral device. B_WRITE is a pseudo flag that occupies the same bit location as B_READ. B_WRITE cannot be directly tested; it is only detected as the NOT form of B_READ.

av_forw and av_back can be used by the driver to link the buffer into driver work lists.

b_dev contains the external major and minor device numbers of the device accessed. For Release 4.0, this field is replaced by the expanded device number field b_edev. b_dev is maintained for compatibility.

b_bcount specifies the number of bytes to be transferred in both a paged and a non-paged I/O request.

b_addr is either the virtual address of the I/O request, or an offset into the first page of a page list depending on whether B_PAGEIO is set. If it is set, the b_pages field of the buffer header will point to a sorted list of page structures and b_addr will be the offset into the first page. If B_PAGEIO is not set, b_addr is the virtual address from which data is read or to which data is written.

b_blkno identifies which logical block on the device (the device is defined by the device number) is to be accessed. The driver may have to convert this logical block number to a physical location such as a cylinder, track, and sector of a disk.

The b_oerror with a char data type and the expanded b_error with an int data type both may hold an error code that should be passed as a return code from your driver routine. b_error and b_oerror is set in conjunction with the B_ERROR flag (set by the operating system in the b_flags member). The error codes are described in Appendix A.

b_resid indicates the number of bytes not transferred because of an error.

b_start holds the time the I/O request was started.

b_proc contains the process table entry address for the process requesting an unbuffered (direct) data transfer to a user data area (this member is set to 0 when the transfer is buffered). The process table entry is used to perform proper virtual to physical address translation of the b_un member.

b_pages contains a pointer to the page structure list used in a paged I/O operation.

b_bufsize contains the size of the allocated buffer.

(*b_iodone) identifies a specific `biodone` routine to be called by the driver when the I/O is complete.

b_vp identifies the vnode associated with the block.

SEE ALSO

strategy(D2DK), physiock(D3D), brelse(D3DK), clrbuf(D3DK), iovec(D4DK), uio(D4DK)

cred (D4DK)   **cred (D4DK)**

NAME
cred – access credential structure

SYNOPSIS
```
#include <sys/cred.h>
```

DESCRIPTION
This structure is used to check the access credentials of the process requesting access to kernel space.

The size of the `cr_groups[]` array is configurable, however, its size is the same for all `cred` structures. Note that `cr_ngroups` records the number of elements currently in use, not the array size.

STRUCTURE MEMBERS
```
ushort  cr_ref;         /* reference count on processes using */
                        /* cred structure.  Not set by drivers. */
ushort  cr_ngroups;     /* number of groups in cr_groups */
uid_t   cr_uid;         /* effective user ID */
gid_t   cr_gid;         /* effective group ID */
uid_t   cr_ruid;        /* real user ID */
gid_t   cr_rgid;        /* real group ID */
uid_t   cr_suid;        /* "saved" user ID (from exec) */
gid_t   cr_sgid;        /* "saved" group ID (from exec) */
gid_t   cr_groups[1];   /* supplementary groups list */
```

The `cred` structure is defined as type `cred_t`.

SEE ALSO
open(D2DK), close(D2DK), ioctl(D2DK), mmap(D2DK), read(D2DK), write(D2DK), segmap(D2DK)

datab (D4DK)

NAME
datab – STREAMS message data structure

SYNOPSIS
```
#include <sys/stream.h>
```

DESCRIPTION
The `datab` structure describes the data of a STREAMS message. The actual data contained in a STREAMS message is stored in a data buffer pointed to by this structure. A `msgb` (message block) structure includes a field that points to a `datab` structure.

A data block can have more than one message block pointing to it at one time, so the `db_ref` member keeps track of a data block's references, preventing it from being deallocated until all message blocks are finished with it.

STRUCTURE MEMBERS
```
union {
    struct datab    *freep;     /* routine to free non-STREAMS buffer */
    struct free_rtn *frtnp;
} db_f;
unsigned char       *db_base;   /* first byte of buffer */
unsigned char       *db_lim;    /* last byte (+1) of buffer */
unsigned char       db_ref;     /* # of message pointers to this data */
unsigned char       db_type;    /* message type */
unsigned char       db_iswhat;  /* status of msg/data/buffer triplet */
unsigned int        db_size;    /* used internally */
caddr_t             db_msgaddr; /* triplet mesg header; points to datab */
long                db_filler;  /* reserved for future use */
```

A `datab` structure is defined as type `dblk_t`.

SEE ALSO
BCI Driver Development Guide, Chapter 4, "Header Files and Data Structures"

free_rtn(D4DK), msgb(D4DK)

free_rtn (D4DK)

NAME
free_rtn – structure that specifies a driver's message freeing routine

SYNOPSIS
#include <sys/stream.h>

DESCRIPTION
The `free_rtn` structure is referenced by the `dp_freep` member of the `datab` structure. When `freeb(D3D)` is called to free the message, the driver's message freeing routine (referenced through the `free_rtn` structure) is called, with arguments, to free the data buffer.

STRUCTURE MEMBERS
```
void    (*free_func)()   /* user's freeing routine */
char    *free_arg        /* arguments to free_func() */
```

The `free_rtn` structure is defined as type `frtn_t`.

SEE ALSO
datab(D4DK), esballoc(D3DK)

hdedata (D4D)

NAME
hdedata – hard disk error data structure

SYNOPSIS
#include <sys/hdelog.h>

DESCRIPTION
The hdedata data structure temporarily stores hard disk error information sent to an error queue. A hdedata structure is initialized for every disk on the system by hdeeqd(D3D) when the system is booted. An error queue is also initialized by hdeeqd.

When the disk driver finds an error, it provides hdelog(D3D) with the error information. hdelog passes the hdedata structure for the error to the error queue. This error queue is a queue of bad block reports that have not been remapped. This queue resides in the kernel and not on the disk.

After a number or errors are accumulated, an administrator examines the list of errors collected in the queue. If any of the errors need to be "fixed," the administrator remaps the bad block. Remapping means that the block address is rewritten to a defect table on the disk. Physical Description sector information points to this defect table.

The following figure illustrates the logging of hard disk errors:

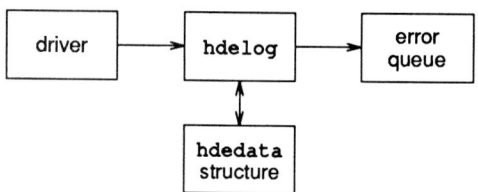

STRUCTURE MEMBERS
```
    o_dev_t   diskdev;        /* Major/minor disk device number */
                              /* (major number for character device) */
    char      dskserno[12];   /* Disk pack serial number (can be all zeros) */
    daddr_t   blkaddr;        /* Physical block address */
                              /* in machine-independent form */
    char      readtype;       /* Error type:CRC (cyclical redundancy check) */
                              /* or ECC (error check and correction) */
    char      severity;       /* Severity type: marginal or unreadable */
    char      badrtcnt;       /* Number of unreadable tries */
    char      bitwidth;       /* Bitwidth of corrected error: 0 if CRC */
    time_t    timestmp;       /* Time stamp */
```

NOTE: The disk pack serial number is not currently evaluated, but it must contain a value. Set to all zeros.

SEE ALSO
hdeeqd(D3D), hdelog(D3D)

iovec(D4DK)   **iovec(D4DK)**

NAME
    iovec – data storage structure for I/O using uio(D4DK)

SYNOPSIS
    #include <sys/uio.h>

DESCRIPTION
    An `iovec` structure describes a data storage area for transfer in a `uio` structure. Conceptually, it may be thought of as a base address and length specification.

STRUCTURE MEMBERS
```
    caddr_t  iov_base;  /* base address of the data storage area */
                        /* represented by the iovec structure */
    int      iov_len;   /* size of the data storage area in bytes */
```

SEE ALSO
    uio(D4DK)

map (D4DK) map (D4DK)

NAME
map – private memory map structure

SYNOPSIS
`#include <sys/map.h>`

DESCRIPTION
The `map` structure defines the size and index into a private space management map. The private map is declared as an instance of the `map` structure using the driver prefix in the form *prefix*map. The size is defined in the `m_size` field as the number of arbitrary units used to make up the map. The index is defined in `m_addr` as the first available unit of the map.

Private maps are managed through a set five functions:

rmalloc	allocates space from a defined and initialized map
rmfree	returns previously allocated space to map
rminit	defines a map structure and initializes a map table
rmwant	returns the number of processes waiting for free space
rmsetwant	increments the count of the number of processes waiting for free space in the map

Private maps can be made up of any units appropriate for the specific uses of the map. For example, units may be byte addresses, pages of memory, or blocks. The map itself does not define the resource, and the size of the map is not related to the size of the `map` structure.

STRUCTURE MEMBERS
```
unsigned long  m_size   /* number of units available */
unsigned long  m_addr   /* address of first available unit */
```

SEE ALSO
rmalloc(D3DK), rmfree(D3DK), rminit(D3DK), rmsetwant(D3DK), rmwant(D3DK)

NAME

module_info – STREAMS driver identification and limit value structure

SYNOPSIS

#include <sys/stream.h>

DESCRIPTION

When a module or driver is declared, several identification and limit values can be set. These values are stored in the module_info structure.

The module_info structure is intended to be read-only. However, the flow control limits (mi_hiwat and mi_lowat) and the packet size limits (mi_minpsz and mi_maxpsz) are copied to the QUEUE structure, where they may be modified.

STRUCTURE MEMBERS

```
ushort  mi_idnum;     /* module ID number */
char    *mi_idname;   /* module name */
short   mi_minpsz;    /* minimum packet size */
short   mi_maxpsz;    /* maximum packet size */
ushort  mi_hiwat;     /* high water mark */
ushort  mi_lowat;     /* low water mark */
```

The constant FMNAMESZ, limiting the length of a module's name, is currently set to a value of eight.

SEE ALSO

queue(D4DK)

msgb (D4DK)

NAME
msgb – STREAMS message block structure

SYNOPSIS
`#include <sys/stream.h>`

DESCRIPTION
A STREAMS message is made up of one or more message blocks, referenced by a pointer to a `msgb` structure. The `b_next` and `b_prev` pointers are used to link messages together on a QUEUE's message queue. The `b_cont` pointer links message blocks together when a message is composed of more than one block.

Each `msgb` structure also includes a pointer to a `datab` structure, the data block (which contains pointers to the actual data of the message), and the type of the message.

STRUCTURE MEMBERS
```
struct msgb     *b_next;    /* next message on queue */
struct msgb     *b_prev;    /* previous message on queue */
struct msgb     *b_cont;    /* next message block */
unsigned char   *b_rptr;    /* 1st unread data byte of buffer */
unsigned char   *b_wptr;    /* 1st unwritten data byte of buffer */
struct datab    *b_datap;   /* pointer to data block */
unsigned char   b_band;     /* message priority */
unsigned char   b_pad1;     /* used internally */
unsigned short  b_flag;     /* used by stream head */
long            b_pad2;     /* used internally */
```

The `msgb` structure is defined as type `mblk_t`.

SEE ALSO
BCI Driver Development Guide, Chapter 4, "Header Files and Data Structures"

datab(D4DK)

qband (D4DK)

NAME
qband – STREAMS queue flow control information structure

SYNOPSIS
#include <sys/stream.h>

DESCRIPTION
The qband structure contains flow control information for each priority band in a queue.

The qband structure is defined as type qband_t.

STRUCTURE MEMBERS
```
struct qband  *qb_next;    /* next band's info */
ulong         qb_count;    /* number of bytes in band */
struct msgb   *qb_first;   /* start of band's data */
struct msgb   *qb_last;    /* end of band's data */
ulong         *qb_hiwat;   /* band's high water mark */
ulong         *qb_lowat;   /* band's low water mark */
ulong         *qb_flag;    /* band's status */
long          *qb_pad1;    /* reserved for future use */
```

SEE ALSO
msgb(D4DK), queue(D4DK)

qinit (D4DK)

NAME
qinit – STREAMS queue processing procedures structure

SYNOPSIS
#include <sys/stream.h>

DESCRIPTION
The `qinit` structure contains pointers to processing procedures for a QUEUE. The `streamtab` structure for the module or driver contains pointers to one `qinit` structure for both upstream and downstream processing.

STRUCTURE MEMBERS

```
int                 (*qi_putp)();      /* put procedure */
int                 (*qi_srvp)();      /* service procedure */
int                 (*qi_qopen)();     /* open procedure */
int                 (*qi_qclose)();    /* close procedure */
int                 (*qi_qadmin)();    /* unused */
struct module_info  *qi_minfo;         /* module parameters */
struct module_stat  *qi_mstat;         /* module statistics */
```

SEE ALSO
BCI Driver Development Guide, Chapter 4, "Header Files and Data Structures"

queue(D4DK), `streamtab`(D4DK)

NAME
queue – STREAMS queue structure

SYNOPSIS
    #include <sys/stream.h>

DESCRIPTION
A STREAMS driver or module consists of two queue structures, one for upstream processing (read) and one for downstream processing (write). This structure is the major building block of a stream. It contains pointers to the processing procedures, pointers to the next and previous queues in the stream, flow control parameters, and a pointer defining the position of its messages on the STREAMS scheduler list.

The queue structure is defined as type queue_t.

STRUCTURE MEMBERS
```
    struct qinit   *q_qinfo;    /* module or driver entry points */
    struct msgb    *q_first;    /* first message in queue */
    struct msgb    *q_last;     /* last message in queue */
    struct queue   *q_next;     /* next queue in stream */
    struct queue   *q_link;     /* used internally */
    _VOID          q_ptr;       /* pointer to private data structure */
    ulong          q_count;     /* approximate size of message queue */
    ulong          q_flag;      /* status of queue */
    long           q_minpsiz;   /* smallest packet accepted by QUEUE */
    long           q_maxpsiz;   /* largest packet accepted by QUEUE */
    ulong          q_hiwat;     /* high water mark */
    ulong          q_lowat;     /* low water mark */
    struct qband   *q_bandp;    /* separate flow info */
    unsigned char  q_nband;     /* number of priority band > 0 */
    unsigned char  q_pad1[3];   /* reserved for future use */
    long           q_pad2[2];   /* reserved for future use */
```

SEE ALSO
msgb(D4DK), qband(D4DK)

NAME

streamtab – STREAMS entity declaration structure

SYNOPSIS

    #include <sys/stream.h>

DESCRIPTION

Each STREAMS driver or module must have a `streamtab` structure. Drivers access this structure through the `cdevsw` table, and modules use the `fmodsw` table.

`streamtab` is made up of `qinit` structures for both the read and write queue portions of each module or driver. (Multiplexing drivers require both upper and lower `qinit` structures.) The `qinit` structure contains the entry points through which the module or driver routines are called.

Normally, the read `QUEUE` contains the `open` and `close` routines. Both the read and write queue can contain `put` and service procedures.

STRUCTURE MEMBERS

    struct qinit   *st_rdinit;   /* read QUEUE */
    struct qinit   *st_wrinit;   /* write QUEUE */
    struct qinit   *st_muxrinit; /* lower read QUEUE*/
    struct qinit   *st_muxwinit; /* lower write QUEUE*/

SEE ALSO

qinit(D4DK)

uio(D4DK)

NAME
uio – scatter/gather I/O request structure

SYNOPSIS
#include <sys/uio.h>

DESCRIPTION
A uio structure describes an I/O request that can be broken up into different data storage areas (scatter/gather I/O). A request is a list of iovec structures (base/length pairs) indicating where in user space or kernel space the I/O data is to be read/written.

The contents of uio structures passed to the driver through the entry points should not be written by the driver. The uiomove(D3D) function takes care of all overhead related to maintaining the state of the uio structure.

STRUCTURE MEMBERS

```
iovec_t   *uio_iov;     /* pointer to the start of the iovec */
                        /* list for the uio structure */
int       uio_iovcnt;   /* the number of iovecs in the list */
off_t     uio_offset;   /* offset into file where data is */
                        /* transferred from or to */
short     uio_segflg;   /* identifies the type of I/O transfer: */
                        /*    UIO_SYSSPACE:  kernel <-> kernel */
                        /*    UIO_USERSPACE: kernel <-> user */
short     uio_fmode;    /* file mode flags (not driver setable) */
daddr_t   uio_limit;    /* ulimit for file (maximum block offset). */
                        /* not driver setable */
int       uio_resid;    /* residual count */
```

The uio_iov member is a pointer to the beginning of the iovec(D4DK) list for the uio. When the uio structure is passed to the driver through an entry point, the driver should not set uio_iov. When the uio structure is created by the driver, uio_iov should be initialized by the driver and not written to afterward.

SEE ALSO
iovec(D4DK)

APPENDIX A: ERROR CODES

APPENDIX A: ERROR CODES

Appendix A: Error Codes

This appendix lists the error codes that should be returned by a driver routine when an error is encountered. Table A-1 lists the error values in alphabetic order. All the error values are defined in /usr/include/sys/errno.h. In the driver open(D2D), close(D2D), ioctl(D2D), read(D2D), and write(D2D) routines, errors are passed back to the user with the return instruction at the end of the routine. In the driver strategy(D2D) routine, errors are passed back to the user by setting the b_error member of the buf(D4D) structure to the error codes.

For STREAMS ioctl routines, error numbers translate to the error numbers sent upstream in an M_IOCNAK message. For STREAMS read and write routines, error numbers translate to the error numbers sent upstream in an M_ERROR message.

NOTE The driver print routine should not return an error code, as the function that it calls, cmn_err(D3D), is declared as void (no error is returned).

Table A-1: Driver Error Codes

Error Value	Error Description	Use in these Driver Routines (D2D)
EAGAIN	Kernel resources, such as the buf structure or cache memory, are not available at this time; cannot open device (device may be busy, or the system resource is not available).	open, ioctl, read, write, strategy
EFAULT	An invalid address has been passed as an argument; memory addressing error.	open, close, ioctl, read, write, strategy
EINTR	PCATCH set, wake with signal; sleep interrupted by signal.	open, close, ioctl, read, write, strategy
EINVAL	An invalid argument was passed to the routine.	open, ioctl, read, write, strategy

Appendix A: Error Codes

Table A-1: Driver Error Codes (continued)

EIO	A device error occurred; a problem was detected in a device status register (the I/O request was valid, but an error occurred on the device).	open, close, ioctl, read, write, strategy
ENXIO	An attempt was made to access a device or subdevice that does not exist (one that is not configured); an attempt was made to perform an invalid I/O operation; an incorrect minor number was specified.	open, close, ioctl, read, write, strategy
EPERM	A process attempting an operation did not have required permission.	open, ioctl, read, write, close
EROFS	An attempt was made to open for writing a read-only device.	open

Table A-2 cross references error values to the driver routines from which the error values can be returned.

Table A-2: Error Codes by Driver Routine

open	close	ioctl	read, write, and strategy
EAGAIN	EFAULT	EAGAIN	EAGAIN
EFAULT	EINTR	EFAULT	EFAULT
EINTR	EIO	EINTR	EINTR
EINVAL	ENXIO	EINVAL	EINVAL
EIO		EIO	EIO
ENXIO		ENXIO	ENXIO
EPERM		EPERM	
EROFS			

APPENDIX B: MIGRATION FROM RELEASE 3.2 TO RELEASE 4.0

APPENDIX B: MIGRATION FROM RELEASE 3.2 TO RELEASE 4.0

Appendix B: Migration from Release 3.2 to Release 4.0

The *UNIX System V Block and Character Interface (BCI) Reference Manual* defined the functions, routines, and structures appropriate for use in the UNIX System V Release 3.2 environment. Table B-1 presents all of the kernel utility functions included in the BCI followed by information about changes to the functions for Release 4.0. Most of the functions fall into one of these categories:

- No change. The function behaves the same way it did in BCI.
- Not supported. The function is not included in either DDI or DKI. No replacement is provided.
- Supported but obsolete. The function is included in DDI or DKI but a replacement is suggested.
- Macro reimplemented as function. The calling and return syntax has not changed for macros converted to functions.
- Replaced. The function is not included in either DDI or DKI but a replacement is provided.
- Renamed only. The function was renamed, but the functionality is the same as it was under the old name.

Appendix B: Migration from Release 3.2 to Release 4.0

Table B-1: 3.2 to 4.0 Migration

BCI	Comments	DDI/DKI
adjmsg	No change	adjmsg
allocb	For memory mapped I/O, use esballoc	allocb
backq	No change	backq
bcopy	No change	bcopy
brelse	Supported but obsolete. Allocate buffer with kmem_alloc or getrbuf(D3DK).	kmem_free or freerbuf
btoc	Replaced	btop, btopr
bufcall	Do not use with esballoc	bufcall
bzero	Word alignment no longer required	bzero
canon	Not supported	None
canput	Use bcanput to test specific priority band	canput
clrbuf	buf structure has changed	clrbuf
cmn_err	No change	cmn_err
copyb	No change	copyb
copyin	Supported but obsolete. Use uiomove	uiomove
copymsg	No change	copymsg
copyout	Supported but obsolete. Use uiomove	uiomove
ctob	Replaced	ptob
datamsg	No change	datamsg
delay	No change	delay
dma_alloc	Not supported	None
dma_breakup	Replaced	dma_pageio
drv_rfile	Not supported	None
dupb	No change	dupb
dupmsg	No change	dupmsg
enableok	Macro reimplemented as function	enableok
flushq	Use flushband to flush specific priority band	flushq

Table B-1: 3.2 to 4.0 Migration (continued)

BCI	Comments	DDI/DKI
freeb	Frees allocb and esballoc allocated buffers	freeb
freemsg	No change	freemsg
fubyte	Replaced	uiomove
fuword	Replaced	uiomove
getc	Not supported	None
getcb	Not supported	None
getcf	Not supported	None
geteblk	Replaced. Use kmem_alloc or getrbuf to allocate a buffer header	kmem_alloc or getrbuf
getq	No change	getq
getvec	No change	getvec
hdeeqd	No change	hdeeqd
hdelog	No change	hdelog
inb	Not supported	None
ind	Not supported	None
insq	No change	insq
iodone	Renamed only	biodone
iomove	Replaced	uiomove
iowait	Renamed only	biowait
kseg	Not supported	None
linkb	No change	linkb
logmsg	Not supported	None
logstray	Not supported	None
longjmp	Not supported	None
major	Renamed. Macro reimplemented as function	getmajor
makedev	Renamed. Macro reimplemented as function	makedevice
malloc	Renamed only	rmalloc
mapinit	Renamed only	rminit
mapwant	Renamed only	rmsetwant

Appendix B: Migration from Release 3.2 to Release 4.0

Table B-1: 3.2 to 4.0 Migration (continued)

BCI	Comments	DDI/DKI
max	No change	max
mfree	Renamed only	rmfree
min	No change	min
minor	Renamed. Macro reimplemented as function	getminor
msgdsize	No change	msgdsize
noenable	Macro reimplemented as function	noenable
OTHERQ	Macro reimplemented as function	OTHERQ
physck	Replaced. Functionality included in physiock	physiock
physio	Replaced. Functionality included in physiock	physiock
psignal	Not supported	None
pullupmsg	No change	pullupmsg
putbq	No change	putbq
putc	Not supported	None
putcb	Not supported	None
putcf	Not supported	None
putctl	No change	putctl
putctl1	No change	putctl1
putnext	Macro reimplemented as function	putnext
putq	No change	putq
qenable	Macro reimplemented as function	qenable
qreply	No change	qreply
qsize	No change	qsize
RD	Macro reimplemented as function	RD
rmvb	No change	rmvb
rmvq	No change	rmvq
signal	Not supported	None
sleep	No change	sleep
spl	No change	spl

Table B-1: 3.2 to 4.0 Migration (continued)

BCI	Comments	DDI/DKI
splx	No change	splx
sptalloc	Not supported	kmem_alloc
sptfree	Not supported	kmem_free
strlog	No change	strlog
subyte	Replaced	uiomove
suser	Replaced	drv_priv
suword	Replaced	uiomove
testb	No change	testb
timeout	No change	timeout
ttclose	Not supported	None
ttin	Not supported	None
ttinit	Not supported	None
ttiocom	Not supported	None
ttioctl	Not supported	None
ttopen	Not supported	None
ttout	Not supported	None
ttread	Not supported	None
ttrstrt	Not supported	None
tttimeo	Not supported	None
ttwrite	Not supported	None
ttyflush	Not supported	None
ttywait	Not supported	None
ttxput	Not supported	None
unkseg	Not supported	None
unlinkb	No change	unlinkb
untimeout	No change	untimeout
useracc	No change	useracc
vtop	No change	vtop
wakeup	No change	wakeup
WR	Macro reimplemented as function	WR

INDEX

INDEX

Index

A

adjmsg(D3DK) 3: 7
allocb(D3DK) 3: 8
  example 3: 9, 23

B

backq(D3DK) 3: 10
bcanput(D3DK) 3: 11
bcopy(D3DK) 3: 12
biodone(D3DK) 3: 14
biowait(D3DK) 3: 16
block I/O 3: 4-6
  buf(D4DK) 4: 3
  iovec(D4DK) 4: 11
  uio(D4DK) 4: 19
bp_mapin(D3DK) 3: 17
bp_mapout(D3DK) 3: 18
brelse(D3DK) 3: 19
btop(D3DK) 3: 20
btopr(D3DK) 3: 21
bufcall(D3DK) 3: 22
  example 3: 22
buf(D4DK) 3: 26, 4: 3
  example 3: 12, 40
buffer header 3: 60, 67
  buf(D4DK) 4: 3
buffers, for raw I/O 3: 6
bzero(D3DK) 3: 24

C

canput(D3DK) 3: 25
  example 3: 22-23, 30, 49
chpoll(D2DK) 2: 4
clock cycles 3: 38

close(D2DK) 2: 6
clrbuf(D3DK) 3: 26
cmn_err(D3DK) 2: 19, 3: 27
  example 3: 28, 38, 64, 100
copyb(D3DK) 3: 30
  example 3: 30
copyin(D3DK) 3: 32
copymsg(D3DK) 3: 33
  example 3: 33
copyout(D3DK) 3: 35
  example 3: 35
CRC (Cyclic Redundancy Check)
  4: 10
cred(D4DK) 4: 7
Cyclic Redundancy Check (CRC)
  4: 10

D

datab(D4DK) 3: 8, 48, 4: 8
  structure members 4: 8
datamsg(D3DK) 3: 37
  example 3: 37
DDI/DKI (Device Driver
    Interface/Driver-Kernel Interface) 1: 1-5
  data structures 4: 1-2
  driver entry point routines 2: 1-3
  error codes A: 1-2
  kernel functions 3: 1-6
  migration from Release 3.2 to
    Release 4.0 B: 1-5
delay(D3DK) 3: 38
  example 3: 38
Device Driver Interface (see
    DDI/DKI)
Direct Memory Access (DMA) 3: 40

Index

DKI (Driver-Kernel Interface) (see DDI/DKI)
DMA (Direct Memory Access) 3: 40
dma_pageio(D3D) 3: 40
  example 3: 40
driver
  block 3: 4-6
  entry points 2: 1-3
  functions 3: 1-6
  porting 1: 2
  STREAMS 3: 2-3
  structures 4: 1-2
Driver-Kernel Interface (see DDI/DKI)
drv_getparm(D3DK) 3: 42
drv_hztousec(D3DK) 3: 44
drv_priv(D3DK) 3: 45
drv_usectohz(D3DK) 3: 46
drv_usecwait(D3DK) 3: 47
dupb(D3DK) 3: 48
  example 3: 49
dupmsg(D3DK) 3: 50
  example 3: 30

E

ECC (Error Check or Correction) 4: 10
enableok(D3DK) 3: 51
  example 3: 51
Error Check or Correction (ECC) 4: 10
esballoc(D3DK) 3: 52
esbbcall(D3DK) 3: 53
etoimajor(D3D) 3: 54

F

flushband(D3DK) 3: 55
flushq(D3DK) 3: 56
  example 3: 56, 106
freeb(D3DK) 3: 58
  example 3: 30, 117, 134
freemsg(D3DK) 3: 59
  example 3: 33, 97, 118
freerbuf(D3DK) 3: 60
free_rtn(D4DK) 4: 9

G

getemajor(D3D) 3: 61
geteminor(D3D) 3: 62
getmajor(D3DK) 3: 64
  example 3: 64
getminor(D3DK) 3: 65
  example 3: 28, 38, 40, 71
getq(D3DK) 3: 66
  example 3: 22, 49, 97
getrbuf(D3DK) 3: 67
getvec(D3D) 3: 68
  example 3: 68

H

hat_getkpfnum(D3K) 3: 69
hdedata(D4D) 4: 10
  example 3: 71, 73
hdeeqd(D3D) 3: 70, 4: 10
  example 3: 71
hdelog(D3D) 3: 73, 4: 10
  example 3: 73
HZ (clock cycles) 3: 38

Index

I

init(D2D) 2: 9
  example 3: 68
insq(D3DK) 3: 76
  example 3: 76
int(D2D) 2: 10
ioctl(D2DK) 2: 12
  example 3: 35
iovec(D4DK) 4: 11
itoemajor(D3D) 3: 78

K

kernel, data copy in 3: 12
kmem_alloc(D3DK) 3: 79
kmem_free(D3DK) 3: 80
kmem_zalloc(D3DK) 3: 81
kvtophys(D3D) 3: 82

L

linkb(D3DK) 3: 83
  example 3: 8, 49

M

major device number 3: 54, 78
  external 3: 61
  internal 3: 64
makedevice(D3DK) 3: 84
map(D4D) 4: 12
max(D3DK) 3: 85
memory, clear 3: 24
message block descriptor 3: 48
message (STREAMS) 3: 8, 11, 25
  block 3: 49, 59

min(D3DK) 3: 86
minor device number
  external 3: 62
  internal 3: 65
mmap(D2K) 2: 16
module_info(D4DK) 4: 13
msgb(D4DK) 3: 8, 48, 4: 14
  example 3: 8, 97, 106, 117–118
msgdsize(D3DK) 3: 87
  example 3: 22

N

noenable(D3DK) 3: 88

O

open(D2DK) 2: 17
OTHERQ(D3DK) 3: 89
  example 3: 89

P

page fault 3: 32
panic 3: 27–28
physiock(D3DK) 3: 92
  example 3: 40
pollwakeup(D3DK) 3: 95
print(D2DK) 2: 19
ptob(D3DK) 3: 96
pullupmsg(D3DK) 3: 97
  example 3: 97
putbq(D3DK) 3: 99
  example 3: 22–23, 49, 130
putctl1(D3DK) 3: 102
  example 3: 100

Index

putctl(D3DK)   3: 100
  example   3: 100
put(D2DK)   2: 20
  example   3: 56
putnext(D3DK)   3: 103
  example   3: 8–9, 22–23, 30, 49, 56
putq(D3DK)   3: 104
  example   3: 37, 76

Q

qband(D4DK)   4: 15
qenable(D3DK)   3: 105
  example   3: 22–23, 49, 51, 130
qinit(D4DK)   4: 16
qreply(D3DK)   3: 106
qsize(D3DK)   3: 108
queue(D4DK)   4: 17
  example   3: 49, 51, 56, 97, 100, 106, 118

R

raw I/O   3: 6
RD(D3DK)   3: 109
  example   3: 8–9, 56, 106
read(D2DK)   2: 22, 3: 35
  example   3: 40
rmalloc(D3DK)   3: 110
  example   3: 112
rmfree(D3DK)   3: 114
rminit(D3DK)   3: 115
rmsetwant(D3DK)   3: 116
  example   3: 112
rmvb(D3DK)   3: 117
  example   3: 117
rmvq(D3DK)   3: 118
  example   3: 118

rmwant(D3DK)   3: 120

S

SAMESTR(D3DK)   3: 121
scatter/gather I/O   4: 19
segmap(D2K)   2: 23
size(D2D)   2: 25
sleep(D3DK)   3: 122
spl(D3D)   3: 125
  during DMA   3: 40
srv(D2DK)   2: 26
  example   3: 22, 130
start(D2D)   2: 28
strategy(D2DK)   2: 29, 4: 3
  example   3: 40
STREAMS entry points   2: 1–3
STREAMS functions   3: 2–3
STREAMS message blocks   3: 8–9, 48, 50, 58–59
STREAMS message queues   3: 10–11, 25, 51
STREAMS messages   3: 7, 33, 37, 55–56, 87
STREAMS structures   4: 1–2
streamtab(D4DK)   4: 18
strlog(D3DK)   3: 127
strqget(D3DK)   3: 128
strqset(D3DK)   3: 129

T

testb(D3DK)   3: 130
  example   3: 130
timeout(D3DK)   3: 132
  example   3: 22–23, 49, 130, 135

U

uio(D4DK)   4: 19
uiomove(D3DK)   3: 133
unlinkb(D3DK)   3: 134
  example   3: 134
untimeout(D3DK)   3: 135
  example   3: 135
ureadc(D3DK)   3: 138
useracc(D3DK)   3: 139
uwritec(D3DK)   3: 140

V

vtop(D3D)   3: 141

W

wakeup(D3DK)   3: 142
  example   3: 135
WR(D3DK)   3: 143
  example   3: 143
write(D2DK)   2: 30, 3: 35
  example   3: 40

PERMUTED INDEX

PERMUTED INDEX

Permuted Index

cred:	access credential structure	cred(D4DK)
close: relinquish	access to a device	close(D2DK)
open: gain	access to a device	open(D2DK)
start: start	access to a device	start(D2D)
useracc: verify whether user has	access to memory	useracc(D3DK)
event sleep: suspend process	activity pending execution of an	sleep(D3DK)
ureadc:	add character to a uio structure	ureadc(D3DK)
vector for a virtual feature card	address getvec: get an interrupt	getvec(D3D)
get page frame number for kernel	address hat_getkpfnum:	hat_getkpfnum(D3K)
virtual address to physical	address kvtophys: convert kernel	kvtophys(D3D)
vtop: convert virtual to physical	address	vtop(D3D)
bcopy: copy data between	address locations in the kernel	bcopy(D3DK)
bp_mapin: allocate virtual	address space	bp_mapin(D3DK)
bp_mapout: deallocate virtual	address space	bp_mapout(D3DK)
kvtophys: convert kernel virtual	address to physical address	kvtophys(D3D)
	adjmsg: trim bytes from a message	adjmsg(D3DK)
allocb:	allocate a message block	allocb(D3DK)
shared buffer esballoc:	allocate a message block using a	esballoc(D3DK)
kernel free memory kmem_zalloc:	allocate and clear space from	kmem_zalloc(D3DK)
space management map rmalloc:	allocate space from a private	rmalloc(D3DK)
memory kmem_alloc:	allocate space from kernel free	kmem_alloc(D3DK)
bp_mapin:	allocate virtual address space	bp_mapin(D3DK)
kmem_free: free previously	allocated kernel memory	kmem_free(D3DK)
allocb: allocate a message block	allocb(D3DK)
testb: check for an	available buffer	testb(D3DK)
a function when a buffer becomes	available bufcall: call	bufcall(D3DK)
call function when buffer is	available esbbcall:	esbbcall(D3DK)
behind the current queue	backq: get pointer to the queue	backq(D3DK)
messages for a specified priority	band flushband: flush	flushband(D3DK)
get information about a queue or	band of the queue strqget:	strqget(D3DK)
information about a queue or	band of the queue /change	strqset(D3DK)
locations in the kernel	bcopy: copy data between address	bcopy(D3DK)
call a function when a buffer	becomes available bufcall:	bufcall(D3DK)
backq: get pointer to the queue	behind the current queue	backq(D3DK)
brelse: return buffer to the	bfreelist	brelse(D3DK)
block I/O and wakeup processes	biodone: release buffer after	biodone(D3DK)
pending completion of block I/O	biowait: suspend processes	biowait(D3DK)
allocb: allocate a message	block	allocb(D3DK)
copyb: copy a message	block	copyb(D3DK)
freeb: free a message	block	freeb(D3DK)
rmvb: remove a message	block from a message	rmvb(D3DK)
unlinkb: remove a message	block from the head of a message	unlinkb(D3DK)
biodone: release buffer after	block I/O and wakeup processes	biodone(D3DK)
buf:	block I/O data transfer structure	buf(D4DK)
processes pending completion of	block I/O biowait: suspend	biowait(D3DK)
strategy: perform	block I/O	strategy(D2DK)
msgb: STREAMS message	block structure	msgb(D4DK)

Permuted Index

esballoc: allocate a message	block using a shared buffer .... esballoc(D3DK)
spl:	block/allow interrupts .... spl(D3D)
linkb: concatenate two message	blocks .... linkb(D3DK)
address space	bp_mapin: allocate virtual .... bp_mapin(D3DK)
address space	bp_mapout: deallocate virtual .... bp_mapout(D3DK)
manageable units dma_pageio:	break up an I/O request into .... dma_pageio(D3DK)
bfreelist	brelse: return buffer to the .... brelse(D3DK)
size in pages (round down)	btop: convert size in bytes to .... btop(D3DK)
size in pages (round up)	btopr: convert size in bytes to .... btopr(D3DK)
structure	buf: block I/O data transfer .... buf(D4DK)
buffer becomes available	bufcall: call a function when a .... bufcall(D3DK)
processes biodone: release	buffer after block I/O and wakeup .... biodone(D3DK)
bufcall: call a function when a	buffer becomes available .... bufcall(D3DK)
clrbuf: erase the contents of a	buffer .... clrbuf(D3DK)
from a user program to a driver	buffer copyin: copy data .... copyin(D3DK)
a message block using a shared	buffer esballoc: allocate .... esballoc(D3DK)
testb: check for an available	buffer .... testb(D3DK)
freerbuf: free a raw	buffer header .... freerbuf(D3DK)
getrbuf: get a raw	buffer header .... getrbuf(D3DK)
esbbcall: call function when	buffer is available .... esbbcall(D3DK)
brelse: return	buffer to the bfreelist .... brelse(D3DK)
drv_usecwait:	busy-wait for specified interval .... drv_usecwait(D3DK)
memory for a given number of	bytes bzero: clear .... bzero(D3DK)
convert size in pages to size in	bytes ptob: .... ptob(D3DK)
adjmsg: trim	bytes from a message .... adjmsg(D3DK)
msgdsize: return the number of	bytes in a message .... msgdsize(D3DK)
pullupmsg: concatenate	bytes in a message .... pullupmsg(D3DK)
down) btop: convert size in	bytes to size in pages (round .... btop(D3DK)
btopr: convert size in	bytes to size in pages (round up) .... btopr(D3DK)
number of bytes	bzero: clear memory for a given .... bzero(D3DK)
becomes available bufcall:	call a function when a buffer .... bufcall(D3DK)
previous timeout(D3DK) function	call untimeout: cancel .... untimeout(D3DK)
available esbbcall:	call function when buffer is .... esbbcall(D3DK)
function call untimeout:	cancel previous timeout(D3DK) .... untimeout(D3DK)
vector for a virtual feature	card address /get an interrupt .... getvec(D3D)
or band of the queue strqset:	change information about a queue .... strqset(D3DK)
ioctl: control a	character device .... ioctl(D2DK)
entry point for a non-STREAMS	character driver chpoll: poll .... chpoll(D2DK)
uwritec: remove a	character from a uio structure .... uwritec(D3DK)
ureadc: add	character to a uio structure .... ureadc(D3DK)
testb:	check for an available buffer .... testb(D3DK)
mapped device mmap:	check virtual mapping for memory .... mmap(D2K)
non-STREAMS character driver	chpoll: poll entry point for a .... chpoll(D2DK)
of bytes bzero:	clear memory for a given number .... bzero(D3DK)
memory kmem_zalloc: allocate and	clear space from kernel free .... kmem_zalloc(D3DK)
for a specified number of	clock ticks /process execution .... delay(D3DK)
convert microseconds to	clock ticks drv_usectohz: .... drv_usectohz(D3DK)

Permuted Index

drv_hztousec: convert	clock ticks to microseconds	drv_hztousec(D3DK)
device	close: relinquish access to a	close(D2DK)
buffer	clrbuf: erase the contents of a	clrbuf(D3DK)
or panic the system	cmn_err: display an error message	cmn_err(D3DK)
suspend processes pending	completion of block I/O biowait:	biowait(D3DK)
pullupmsg:	concatenate bytes in a message	pullupmsg(D3DK)
linkb:	concatenate two message blocks	linkb(D3DK)
a driver message on system	console print: display	print(D2DK)
clrbuf: erase the	contents of a buffer	clrbuf(D3DK)
ioctl:	control a character device	ioctl(D2DK)
qband: STREAMS queue flow	control information structure	qband(D4DK)
putctl: send a	control message to a queue	putctl(D3DK)
parameter to a/ putctl1: send a	control message with a one-byte	putctl1(D3DK)
microseconds drv_hztousec:	convert clock ticks to	drv_hztousec(D3DK)
internal major number etoimajor:	convert external major number to	etoimajor(D3D)
major device number itoemajor:	convert internal to external	itoemajor(D3D)
physical address kvtophys:	convert kernel virtual address to	kvtophys(D3D)
ticks drv_usectohz:	convert microseconds to clock	drv_usectohz(D3D)
structure page_numtopp:	convert page frame number to page	
		page_numtopp(D3DK)
frame number page_pptonum:	convert page structure to page	page_pptonum(D3DK)
pages (round down) btop:	convert size in bytes to size in	btop(D3DK)
pages (round up) btopr:	convert size in bytes to size in	btopr(D3DK)
bytes ptob:	convert size in pages to size in	ptob(D3DK)
address vtop:	convert virtual to physical	vtop(D3D)
copyb:	copy a message block	copyb(D3DK)
copymsg:	copy a message	copymsg(D3DK)
locations in the kernel bcopy:	copy data between address	bcopy(D3DK)
program copyout:	copy data from a driver to a user	copyout(D3DK)
a driver buffer copyin:	copy data from a user program to	copyin(D3DK)
structure uiomove:	copy kernel data using uio(D4DK)	uiomove(D3DK)
	copyb: copy a message block	copyb(D3DK)
program to a driver buffer	copyin: copy data from a user	copyin(D3DK)
	copymsg: copy a message	copymsg(D3DK)
to a user program	copyout: copy data from a driver	copyout(D3DK)
	cred: access credential structure	cred(D4DK)
cred: access	credential structure	cred(D4DK)
pointer to the queue behind the	current queue backq: get	backq(D3DK)
the kernel bcopy: copy	data between address locations in	bcopy(D3DK)
read: read	data from a device	read(D2DK)
program copyout: copy	data from a driver to a user	copyout(D3DK)
driver buffer copyin: copy	data from a user program to a	copyin(D3DK)
test whether a message is a	data message datamsg:	datamsg(D3DK)
using uio(D4DK) iovec:	data storage structure for I/O	iovec(D4DK)
datab: STREAMS message	data structure	datab(D4DK)
hdedata: hard disk error	data structure	hdedata(D4D)
write: write	data to a device	write(D2DK)

Permuted Index 3

Permuted Index

buf: block I/O	data transfer structure .... buf(D4DK)
uiomove: copy kernel	data using uio(D4DK) structure .... uiomove(D3DK)
structure	datab: STREAMS message data .... datab(D4DK)
is a data message	datamsg: test whether a message .... datamsg(D3DK)
bp_mapout:	deallocate virtual address space ..... bp_mapout(D3DK)
streamtab: STREAMS entity	declaration structure .... streamtab(D4DK)
for a specified number of clock/	delay: delay process execution .... delay(D3DK)
specified number of clock/ delay:	delay process execution for a .... delay(D3DK)
drv_priv:	determine driver privilege .... drv_priv(D3DK)
close: relinquish access to a	device .... close(D2DK)
init: initialize a	device .... init(D2D)
ioctl: control a character	device .... ioctl(D2DK)
virtual mapping for memory mapped	device mmap: check .... mmap(D2K)
open: gain access to a	device .... open(D2DK)
read: read data from a	device .... read(D2DK)
size: return size of logical	device .... size(D2D)
start: start access to a	device .... start(D2D)
write: write data to a	device .... write(D2DK)
int: process a	device interrupt .... int(D2D)
segmap: map	device memory into user space .... segmap(D2K)
getemajor: get external major	device number .... getemajor(D3D)
geteminor: get external minor	device number .... geteminor(D3D)
get major or internal major	device number getmajor: .... getmajor(D3D)
get minor or internal minor	device number getminor: .... getminor(D3D)
internal to external major	device number itoemajor: convert ...... itoemajor(D3D)
and minor makedevice: make	device number from external major .... makedevice(D3DK)
on a stream in the reverse	direction qreply: send a message .... qreply(D3DK)
hdedata: hard	disk error data structure .... hdedata(D4D)
hdelog: log hard	disk error .... hdelog(D3D)
hdeeqd: initialize hard	disk error logging .... hdeeqd(D3D)
system console print:	display a driver message on .... print(D2DK)
the system cmn_err:	display an error message or panic ..... cmn_err(D3DK)
request into manageable units	dma_pageio: break up an I/O .... dma_pageio(D3D)
in bytes to size in pages (round	down) btop: convert size .... btop(D3DK)
data from a user program to a	driver buffer copyin: copy .... copyin(D3DK)
point for a non-STREAMS character	driver chpoll: poll entry .... chpoll(D2DK)
submit messages to the log	driver strlog: .... strlog(D3DK)
write queue for this module or	driver WR: get pointer to the .... WR(D3DK)
value/ module_info: STREAMS	driver identification and limit ..... module_info(D4DK)
print: display a	driver message on system console .... print(D2DK)
drv_priv: determine	driver privilege .... drv_priv(D3DK)
copyout: copy data from a	driver to a user program .... copyout(D3DK)
/structure that specifies a	driver's message freeing routine .... free_rtn(D4DK)
state information	drv_getparm: retrieve kernel .... drv_getparm(D3DK)
to microseconds	drv_hztousec: convert clock ticks ...... drv_hztousec(D3DK)
privilege	drv_priv: determine driver .... drv_priv(D3DK)
microseconds to clock ticks	drv_usectohz: convert .... drv_usectohz(D3DK)

4

DDI/DKI Reference Manual

Permuted Index

specified interval	drv_usecwait: busy-wait for	drv_usecwait(D3DK)
dupmsg:	duplicate a message	dupmsg(D3DK)
	dupmsg: duplicate a message	dupmsg(D3DK)
qenable:	enable a queue	qenable(D3DK)
service	enableok: reschedule a queue for	enableok(D3DK)
streamtab: STREAMS	entity declaration structure	streamtab(D4DK)
character driver chpoll: poll	entry point for a non-STREAMS	chpoll(D2DK)
clrbuf:	erase the contents of a buffer	clrbuf(D3DK)
hdedata: hard disk	error data structure	hdedata(D4D)
geterror: return I/O	error	geterror(D3DK)
hdelog: log hard disk	error	hdelog(D3D)
hdeeqd: initialize hard disk	error logging	hdeeqd(D3D)
cmn_err: display an	error message or panic the system	cmn_err(D3DK)
block using a shared buffer	esballoc: allocate a message	esballoc(D3DK)
buffer is available	esbbcall: call function when	esbbcall(D3DK)
number to internal major number	etoimajor: convert external major	etoimajor(D3D)
activity pending execution of an	event sleep: suspend process	sleep(D3DK)
inform a process that an	event has occurred pollwakeup:	pollwakeup(D3DK)
specified length of/ timeout:	execute a function after a	timeout(D3DK)
wakeup: resume suspended process	execution	wakeup(D3DK)
of clock/ delay: delay process	execution for a specified number	delay(D3DK)
suspend process activity pending	execution of an event sleep:	sleep(D3DK)
/make device number from	external major and minor	makedevice(D3DK)
getemajor: get	external major device number	getemajor(D3D)
itoemajor: convert internal to	external major device number	itoemajor(D3D)
major number etoimajor: convert	external major number to internal	etoimajor(D3D)
geteminor: get	external minor device number	geteminor(D3D)
an interrupt vector for a virtual	feature card address getvec: get	getvec(D3D)
queue qsize:	find the number of messages on a	qsize(D3DK)
rmsetwant: set the map's wait	flag for a wakeup	rmsetwant(D3DK)
structure qband: STREAMS queue	flow control information	qband(D4DK)
priority band flushband:	flush messages for a specified	flushband(D3DK)
specified priority band	flushband: flush messages for a	flushband(D3DK)
queue	flushq: remove messages from a	flushq(D3DK)
convert page structure to page	frame number page_pptonum:	page_pptonum(D3DK)
hat_getkpfnum: get page	frame number for kernel address	hat_getkpfnum(D3K)
page_numtopp: convert page	frame number to page structure	page_numtopp(D3DK)
freeb:	free a message block	freeb(D3DK)
freerbuf:	free a raw buffer header	freerbuf(D3DK)
allocate space from kernel	free memory kmem_alloc:	kmem_alloc(D3DK)
and clear space from kernel	free memory /allocate	kmem_zalloc(D3DK)
rmwant: wait for	free memory	rmwant(D3DK)
memory kmem_free:	free previously allocated kernel	kmem_free(D3DK)
space management map rmfree:	free space back into a private	rmfree(D3DK)
	freeb: free a message block	freeb(D3DK)
that specifies a driver's message	freeing routine /structure	free_rtn(D4DK)
header	freerbuf: free a raw buffer	freerbuf(D3DK)

Permuted Index

specifies a driver's message/	free_rtn: structure that	free_rtn(D4DK)
of time timeout: execute a	function after a specified length	timeout(D3DK)
cancel previous timeout(D3DK)	function call untimeout:	untimeout(D3DK)
available bufcall: call a	function when a buffer becomes	bufcall(D3DK)
esbbcall: call	function when buffer is available	esbbcall(D3DK)
open:	gain access to a device	open(D2DK)
device number	getmajor: get external major	getmajor(D3D)
device number	geteminor: get external minor	geteminor(D3D)
	geterror: return I/O error	geterror(D3D)
major device number	getmajor: get major or internal	getmajor(D3DK)
minor device number	getminor: get minor or internal	getminor(D3DK)
queue	getq: get the next message from a	getq(D3DK)
	getrbuf: get a raw buffer header	getrbuf(D3DK)
for a virtual feature card/	getvec: get an interrupt vector	getvec(D3D)
bzero: clear memory for a	given number of bytes	bzero(D3DK)
hdedata:	hard disk error data structure	hdedata(D4D)
hdelog: log	hard disk error	hdelog(D3D)
hdeeqd: initialize	hard disk error logging	hdeeqd(D3D)
number for kernel address	hat_getkpfnum: get page frame	hat_getkpfnum(D3K)
structure	hdedata: hard disk error data	hdedata(D4D)
error logging	hdeeqd: initialize hard disk	hdeeqd(D3D)
	hdelog: log hard disk error	hdelog(D3D)
remove a message block from the	head of a message unlinkb:	unlinkb(D3DK)
putbq: place a message at the	head of a queue	putbq(D3DK)
freerbuf: free a raw buffer	header	freerbuf(D3DK)
getrbuf: get a raw buffer	header	getrbuf(D3DK)
module_info: STREAMS driver	identification and limit value/	module_info(D4DK)
has occurred pollwakeup:	inform a process that an event	pollwakeup(D3DK)
of the queue strqget: get	information about a queue or band	strqget(D3DK)
of the queue strqset: change	information about a queue or band	strqset(D3DK)
retrieve kernel state	information drv_getparm:	drv_getparm(D3DK)
qband: STREAMS queue flow control	information structure	qband(D4DK)
	init: initialize a device	init(D2D)
init:	initialize a device	init(D2D)
management map rminit:	initialize a private space	rminit(D3DK)
logging hdeeqd:	initialize hard disk error	hdeeqd(D3D)
insq:	insert a message into a queue	insq(D3DK)
queue	insq: insert a message into a	insq(D3DK)
	int: process a device interrupt	int(D2D)
max: return the larger of two	integers	max(D3DK)
min: return the lesser of two	integers	min(D3DK)
getmajor: get major or	internal major device number	getmajor(D3DK)
convert external major number to	internal major number etoimajor:	etoimajor(D3D)
getminor: get minor or	internal minor device number	getminor(D3DK)
number itoemajor: convert	internal to external major device	itoemajor(D3D)
int: process a device	interrupt	int(D2D)
feature card/ getvec: get an	interrupt vector for a virtual	getvec(D3D)

Permuted Index

spl: block/allow	interrupts .... spl(D3D)
busy-wait for specified	interval drv_usecwait: .... drv_usecwait(D3DK)
/release buffer after block	I/O and wakeup processes .... biodone(D3DK)
buf: block	I/O data transfer structure .... buf(D4DK)
geterror: return	I/O error .... geterror(D3DK)
pending completion of block	I/O biowait: suspend processes .... biowait(D3DK)
strategy: perform block	I/O .... strategy(D2DK)
physiock: validate and issue raw	I/O request .... physiock(D3D)
dma_pageio: break up an	I/O request into manageable units .... dma_pageio(D3D)
uio: scatter/gather	I/O request structure .... uio(D4DK)
iovec: data storage structure for	I/O using uio(D4DK) .... iovec(D4DK)
	ioctl: control a character device .... ioctl(D2DK)
I/O using uio(D4DK)	iovec: data storage structure for .... iovec(D4DK)
physiock: validate and	issue raw I/O request .... physiock(D3D)
external major device number	itoemajor: convert internal to .... itoemajor(D3D)
get page frame number for	kernel address hat_getkpfnum: .... hat_getkpfnum(D3K)
structure uiomove: copy	kernel data using uio(D4DK) .... uiomove(D3DK)
between address locations in the	kernel bcopy: copy data .... bcopy(D3DK)
kmem_alloc: allocate space from	kernel free memory .... kmem_alloc(D3DK)
allocate and clear space from	kernel free memory kmem_zalloc: .... kmem_zalloc(D3DK)
free previously allocated	kernel memory kmem_free: .... kmem_free(D3DK)
drv_getparm: retrieve	kernel state information .... drv_getparm(D3DK)
physical/ kvtophys: convert	kernel virtual address to .... kvtophys(D3D)
kernel free memory	kmem_alloc: allocate space from .... kmem_alloc(D3DK)
allocated kernel memory	kmem_free: free previously .... kmem_free(D3DK)
space from kernel free memory	kmem_zalloc: allocate and clear .... kmem_zalloc(D3DK)
address to physical address	kvtophys: convert kernel virtual .... kvtophys(D3D)
max: return the	larger of two integers .... max(D3DK)
a function after a specified	length of time timeout: execute .... timeout(D3DK)
min: return the	lesser of two integers .... min(D3DK)
/STREAMS driver identification and	limit value structure .... module_info(D4DK)
blocks	linkb: concatenate two message .... linkb(D3DK)
bcopy: copy data between address	locations in the kernel .... bcopy(D3DK)
strlog: submit messages to the	log driver .... strlog(D3DK)
hdelog:	log hard disk error .... hdelog(D3D)
initialize hard disk error	logging hdeeqd: .... hdeeqd(D3D)
size: return size of	logical device .... size(D2D)
make device number from external	major and minor makedevice: .... makedevice(D3DK)
getemajor: get external	major device number .... getemajor(D3DK)
getmajor: get major or internal	major device number .... getmajor(D3DK)
convert internal to external	major device number itoemajor: .... itoemajor(D3D)
external major number to internal	major number etoimajor: convert .... etoimajor(D3D)
etoimajor: convert external	major number to internal major/ .... etoimajor(D3D)
number getmajor: get	major or internal major device .... getmajor(D3DK)
from external major and minor	makedevice: make device number .... makedevice(D3DK)
break up an I/O request into	manageable units dma_pageio: .... dma_pageio(D3D)
space from a private space	management map rmalloc: allocate .... rmalloc(D3DK)

Permuted Index

space back into a private space	management map rmfree: free .... rmfree(D3DK)
initialize a private space	management map rminit: .... rminit(D3DK)
segmap:	map device memory into user space .... segmap(D2K)
from a private space management	map rmalloc: allocate space .... rmalloc(D3DK)
into a private space management	map rmfree: free space back .... rmfree(D3DK)
a private space management	map rminit: initialize .... rminit(D3DK)
	map: private memory map structure .... map(D4DK)
map: private memory	map structure .... map(D4DK)
check virtual mapping for memory	mapped device mmap: .... mmap(D2K)
mmap: check virtual	mapping for memory mapped device .... mmap(D2K)
rmsetwant: set the	map's wait flag for a wakeup .... rmsetwant(D3DK)
integers	max: return the larger of two .... max(D3DK)
allocate space from kernel free	memory kmem_alloc: .... kmem_alloc(D3DK)
free previously allocated kernel	memory kmem_free: .... kmem_free(D3DK)
and clear space from kernel free	memory kmem_zalloc: allocate .... kmem_zalloc(D3DK)
rmwant: wait for free	memory .... rmwant(D3DK)
verify whether user has access to	memory useracc: .... useracc(D3DK)
bytes bzero: clear	memory for a given number of .... bzero(D3DK)
segmap: map device	memory into user space .... segmap(D2K)
map: private	memory map structure .... map(D4DK)
mmap: check virtual mapping for	memory mapped device .... mmap(D2K)
putbq: place a	message at the head of a queue .... putbq(D3DK)
allocb: allocate a	message block .... allocb(D3DK)
copyb: copy a	message block .... copyb(D3DK)
freeb: free a	message block .... freeb(D3DK)
rmvb: remove a	message block from a message .... rmvb(D3DK)
message unlinkb: remove a	message block from the head of a .... unlinkb(D3DK)
msgb: STREAMS	message block structure .... msgb(D4DK)
buffer esballoc: allocate a	message block using a shared .... esballoc(D3DK)
linkb: concatenate two	message blocks .... linkb(D3DK)
datab: STREAMS	message data structure .... datab(D4DK)
adjmsg: trim bytes from a	message .... adjmsg(D3DK)
copymsg: copy a	message .... copymsg(D3DK)
test whether a message is a data	message datamsg: .... datamsg(D3DK)
dupmsg: duplicate a	message .... dupmsg(D3DK)
return the number of bytes in a	message msgdsize: .... msgdsize(D3DK)
pullupmsg: concatenate bytes in a	message .... pullupmsg(D3DK)
remove a message block from a	message rmvb: .... rmvb(D3DK)
message block from the head of a	message unlinkb: remove a .... unlinkb(D3DK)
/that specifies a driver's	message freeing routine .... free_rtn(D4DK)
getq: get the next	message from a queue .... getq(D3DK)
rmvq: remove a	message from a queue .... rmvq(D3DK)
insq: insert a	message into a queue .... insq(D3DK)
datamsg: test whether a	message is a data message .... datamsg(D3DK)
putq: put a	message on a queue .... putq(D3DK)
reverse direction qreply: send a	message on a stream in the .... qreply(D3DK)
print: display a driver	message on system console .... print(D2DK)

Permuted Index

cmn_err: display an error message or panic the system	cmn_err(D3DK)
putctl: send a control message to a queue	putctl(D3DK)
putnext: send a message to the next queue	putnext(D3DK)
to a/ putctl1: send a control message with a one-byte parameter	putctl1(D3DK)
srv: service queued messages	srv(D2DK)
band flushband: flush messages for a specified priority	flushband(D3DK)
flushq: remove messages from a queue	flushq(D3DK)
put: receive messages from the preceding queue	put(D2DK)
qsize: find the number of messages on a queue	qsize(D3DK)
strlog: submit messages to the log driver	strlog(D3DK)
convert clock ticks to microseconds drv_hztousec:	drv_hztousec(D3DK)
drv_usectohz: convert microseconds to clock ticks	drv_usectohz(D3DK)
integers min: return the lesser of two	min(D3DK)
geteminor: get external minor device number	geteminor(D3D)
getminor: get minor or internal minor device number	getminor(D3DK)
number from external major and minor makedevice: make device	makedevice(D3DK)
number getminor: get minor or internal minor device	getminor(D3DK)
memory mapped device mmap: check virtual mapping for	mmap(D2K)
to the write queue for this module or driver WR: get pointer	WR(D3DK)
identification and limit value/ module_info: STREAMS driver	module_info(D4DK)
structure msgb: STREAMS message block	msgb(D4DK)
bytes in a message msgdsize: return the number of	msgdsize(D3DK)
getq: get the next message from a queue	getq(D3DK)
putnext: send a message to the next queue	putnext(D3DK)
SAMESTR: test if next queue is same type	SAMESTR(D3DK)
being scheduled noenable: prevent a queue from	noenable(D3DK)
chpoll: poll entry point for a non-STREAMS character driver	chpoll(D2DK)
major number to internal major number /convert external	ctoimajor(D3D)
get external major device number getemajor:	getemajor(D3D)
get external minor device number geteminor:	geteminor(D3D)
major or internal major device number getmajor: get	getmajor(D3DK)
minor or internal minor device number getminor: get	getminor(D3DK)
internal to external major device number itoemajor: convert	itoemajor(D3D)
page structure to page frame number page_pptonum: convert	page_pptonum(D3DK)
hat_getkpfnum: get page frame number for kernel address	hat_getkpfnum(D3K)
minor makedevice: make device number from external major and	makedevice(D3DK)
bzero: clear memory for a given number of bytes	bzero(D3DK)
msgdsize: return the number of bytes in a message	msgdsize(D3DK)
process execution for a specified number of clock ticks /delay	delay(D3DK)
qsize: find the number of messages on a queue	qsize(D3DK)
etoimajor: convert external major number to internal major number	etoimajor(D3D)
page_numtopp: convert page frame number to page structure	page_numtopp(D3DK)
a process that an event has occurred pollwakeup: inform	pollwakeup(D3DK)
/send a control message with a one-byte parameter to a queue	putctl1(D3DK)
open: gain access to a device	open(D2DK)
partner queue OTHERQ: get pointer to queue's	OTHERQ(D3DK)

Permuted Index

convert page structure to page frame number page_pptonum:	.... page_pptonum(D3DK)
address hat_getkpfnum: get page frame number for kernel	.... hat_getkpfnum(D3K)
structure page_numtopp: convert page frame number to page	.... page_numtopp(D3DK)
convert page frame number to page structure page_numtopp:	.... page_numtopp(D3DK)
number page_pptonum: convert page structure to page frame	.... page_pptonum(D3DK)
number to page structure page_numtopp: convert page frame	
	.... page_numtopp(D3DK)
structure to page frame number page_pptonum: convert page	.... page_pptonum(D3DK)
convert size in bytes to size in pages (round down) btop:	.... btop(D3DK)
convert size in bytes to size in pages (round up) btopr:	.... btopr(D3DK)
ptob: convert size in pages to size in bytes	.... ptob(D3DK)
display an error message or panic the system cmn_err:	.... cmn_err(D3DK)
a control message with a one-byte parameter to a queue /send	.... putctl1(D3DK)
OTHERQ: get pointer to queue's partner queue	.... OTHERQ(D3DK)
biowait: suspend processes pending completion of block I/O	.... biowait(D3DK)
sleep: suspend process activity pending execution of an event	.... sleep(D3DK)
strategy: perform block I/O	.... strategy(D2DK)
convert kernel virtual address to physical address kvtophys:	.... kvtophys(D3D)
vtop: convert virtual to physical address	.... vtop(D3D)
I/O request physiock: validate and issue raw	.... physiock(D3D)
queue putbq: place a message at the head of a	.... putbq(D3DK)
driver chpoll: poll entry point for a non-STREAMS character	.... chpoll(D2DK)
OTHERQ: get pointer to queue's partner queue	.... OTHERQ(D3DK)
current queue backq: get pointer to the queue behind the	.... backq(D3DK)
RD: get pointer to the read queue	.... RD(D3DK)
this module or driver WR: get pointer to the write queue for	.... WR(D3DK)
non-STREAMS character/ chpoll: poll entry point for a	.... chpoll(D2DK)
an event has occurred pollwakeup: inform a process that	.... pollwakeup(D3DK)
put: receive messages from the preceding queue	.... put(D2DK)
scheduled noenable: prevent a queue from being	.... noenable(D3DK)
call untimeout: cancel previous timeout(D3DK) function	.... untimeout(D3DK)
memory kmem_free: free previously allocated kernel	.... kmem_free(D3DK)
on system console print: display a driver message	.... print(D2DK)
flush messages for a specified priority band flushband:	.... flushband(D3DK)
map: private memory map structure	.... map(D4DK)
rmalloc: allocate space from a private space management map	.... rmalloc(D3DK)
rmfree: free space back into a private space management map	.... rmfree(D3DK)
rminit: initialize a private space management map	.... rminit(D3DK)
drv_priv: determine driver privilege	.... drv_priv(D3DK)
qinit: STREAMS queue processing procedures structure	.... qinit(D4DK)
int: process a device interrupt	.... int(D2D)
execution of an/ sleep: suspend process activity pending	.... sleep(D3DK)
wakeup: resume suspended process execution	.... wakeup(D3DK)
number of clock/ delay: delay process execution for a specified	.... delay(D3DK)
occurred pollwakeup: inform a process that an event has	.... pollwakeup(D3DK)
buffer after block I/O and wakeup processes biodone: release	.... biodone(D3DK)

Permuted Index

block I/O biowait: suspend	processes pending completion of	biowait(D3DK)
qinit: STREAMS queue	processing procedures structure	qinit(D4DK)
copy data from a driver to a user	program copyout:	copyout(D3DK)
copyin: copy data from a user	program to a driver buffer	copyin(D3DK)
size in bytes	ptob: convert size in pages to	ptob(D3DK)
message	pullupmsg: concatenate bytes in a	pullupmsg(D3DK)
putq:	put a message on a queue	putq(D3DK)
preceding queue	put: receive messages from the	put(D2DK)
head of a queue	putbq: place a message at the	putbq(D3DK)
a queue	putctl: send a control message to	putctl(D3DK)
with a one-byte parameter to a/	putctl1: send a control message	putctl1(D3DK)
next queue	putnext: send a message to the	putnext(D3DK)
	putq: put a message on a queue	putq(D3DK)
information structure	qband: STREAMS queue flow control	qband(D4DK)
	qenable: enable a queue	qenable(D3DK)
procedures structure	qinit: STREAMS queue processing	qinit(D4DK)
stream in the reverse direction	qreply: send a message on a	qreply(D3DK)
messages on a queue	qsize: find the number of	qsize(D3DK)
backq: get pointer to the	queue behind the current queue	backq(D3DK)
to the queue behind the current	queue backq: get pointer	backq(D3DK)
flushq: remove messages from a	queue	flushq(D3DK)
getq: get the next message from a	queue	getq(D3DK)
insq: insert a message into a	queue	insq(D3DK)
get pointer to queue's partner	queue OTHERQ:	OTHERQ(D3DK)
place a message at the head of a	queue putbq:	putbq(D3DK)
with a one-byte parameter to a	queue /send a control message	putctl1(D3DK)
send a control message to a	queue putctl:	putctl(D3DK)
messages from the preceding	queue put: receive	put(D2DK)
send a message to the next	queue putnext:	putnext(D3DK)
putq: put a message on a	queue	putq(D3DK)
qenable: enable a	queue	qenable(D3DK)
find the number of messages on a	queue qsize:	qsize(D3DK)
RD: get pointer to the read	queue	RD(D3DK)
rmvq: remove a message from a	queue	rmvq(D3DK)
about a queue or band of the	queue strqget: get information	strqget(D3DK)
about a queue or band of the	queue /change information	strqset(D3DK)
structure qband: STREAMS	queue flow control information	qband(D4DK)
enableok: reschedule a	queue for service	enableok(D3DK)
WR: get pointer to the write	queue for this module or driver	WR(D3DK)
noenable: prevent a	queue from being scheduled	noenable(D3DK)
SAMESTR: test if next	queue is same type	SAMESTR(D3DK)
strqget: get information about a	queue or band of the queue	strqget(D3DK)
/change information about a	queue or band of the queue	strqset(D3DK)
structure qinit: STREAMS	queue processing procedures	qinit(D4DK)
	queue: STREAMS queue structure	queue(D4DK)
queue: STREAMS	queue structure	queue(D4DK)
srv: service	queued messages	srv(D2DK)

Permuted Index

OTHERQ: get pointer to	queue's partner queue .... OTHERQ(D3DK)
freerbuf: free a	raw buffer header .... freerbuf(D3DK)
getrbuf: get a	raw buffer header .... getrbuf(D3DK)
physiock: validate and issue	raw I/O request .... physiock(D3D)
	RD: get pointer to the read queue .... RD(D3DK)
read:	read data from a device .... read(D2DK)
RD: get pointer to the	read queue .... RD(D3DK)
	read: read data from a device .... read(D2DK)
preceding queue put:	receive messages from the .... put(D2DK)
and wakeup processes biodone:	release buffer after block I/O .... biodone(D3DK)
close:	relinquish access to a device .... close(D2DK)
structure uwritec:	remove a character from a uio .... uwritec(D3DK)
message rmvb:	remove a message block from a .... rmvb(D3DK)
head of a message unlinkb:	remove a message block from the .... unlinkb(D3DK)
rmvq:	remove a message from a queue .... rmvq(D3DK)
flushq:	remove messages from a queue .... flushq(D3DK)
validate and issue raw I/O	request physiock: .... physiock(D3D)
dma_pageio: break up an I/O	request into manageable units .... dma_pageio(D3D)
uio: scatter/gather I/O	request structure .... uio(D4DK)
enableok:	reschedule a queue for service .... enableok(D3DK)
execution wakeup:	resume suspended process .... wakeup(D3DK)
drv_getparm:	retrieve kernel state information .... drv_getparm(D3DK)
brelse:	return buffer to the bfreelist .... brelse(D3DK)
geterror:	return I/O error .... geterror(D3DK)
size:	return size of logical device .... size(D2D)
max:	return the larger of two integers .... max(D3DK)
min:	return the lesser of two integers .... min(D3DK)
message msgdsize:	return the number of bytes in a .... msgdsize(D3DK)
send a message on a stream in the	reverse direction qreply: .... qreply(D3DK)
private space management map	rmalloc: allocate space from a .... rmalloc(D3DK)
private space management map	rmfree: free space back into a .... rmfree(D3DK)
space management map	rminit: initialize a private .... rminit(D3DK)
flag for a wakeup	rmsetwant: set the map's wait .... rmsetwant(D3DK)
a message	rmvb: remove a message block from .... rmvb(D3DK)
queue	rmvq: remove a message from a .... rmvq(D3DK)
	rmwant: wait for free memory .... rmwant(D3DK)
size in bytes to size in pages	(round down) btop: convert .... btop(D3DK)
size in bytes to size in pages	(round up) btopr: convert .... btopr(D3DK)
a driver's message freeing	routine /structure that specifies .... free_rtn(D4DK)
same type	SAMESTR: test if next queue is .... SAMESTR(D3DK)
structure uio:	scatter/gather I/O request .... uio(D4DK)
prevent a queue from being	scheduled noenable: .... noenable(D3DK)
user space	segmap: map device memory into .... segmap(D2K)
putctl:	send a control message to a queue .... putctl(D3DK)
one-byte parameter to a/ putctl1:	send a control message with a .... putctl1(D3DK)
reverse direction qreply:	send a message on a stream in the .... qreply(D3DK)
putnext:	send a message to the next queue .... putnext(D3DK)

DDI/DKI Reference Manual

Permuted Index

enableok: reschedule a queue for srv:	service .... enableok(D3DK)
wakeup rmsetwant:	service queued messages .... srv(D2DK)
allocate a message block using a	set the map's wait flag for a .... rmsetwant(D3DK)
ptob: convert size in pages to	shared buffer esballoc: .... esballoc(D3DK)
(round down) btop: convert	size in bytes .... ptob(D3DK)
(round up) btopr: convert	size in bytes to size in pages .... btop(D3DK)
btop: convert size in bytes to	size in bytes to size in pages .... btopr(D3DK)
btopr: convert size in bytes to	size in pages (round down) .... btop(D3DK)
ptob: convert	size in pages (round up) .... btopr(D3DK)
size: return	size in pages to size in bytes .... ptob(D3DK)
device	size of logical device .... size(D2D)
pending execution of an event	size: return size of logical .... size(D2D)
management map rmfree: free	sleep: suspend process activity .... sleep(D3DK)
allocate virtual address	space back into a private space .... rmfree(D3DK)
deallocate virtual address	space bp_mapin: .... bp_mapin(D3DK)
map device memory into user	space bp_mapout: .... bp_mapout(D3DK)
management map rmalloc: allocate	space segmap: .... segmap(D2K)
kmem_alloc: allocate	space from a private space .... rmalloc(D3DK)
kmem_zalloc: allocate and clear	space from kernel free memory .... kmem_alloc(D3DK)
allocate space from a private	space from kernel free memory .... kmem_zalloc(D3DK)
free space back into a private	space management map rmalloc: .... rmalloc(D3DK)
rminit: initialize a private	space management map rmfree: .... rmfree(D3DK)
drv_usecwait: busy-wait for	space management map .... rminit(D3DK)
/execute a function after a	specified interval .... drv_usecwait(D3DK)
/delay process execution for a	specified length of time .... timeout(D3DK)
flushband: flush messages for a	specified number of clock ticks .... delay(D3DK)
freeing/ free_rtn: structure that	specified priority band .... flushband(D3DK)
	specifies a driver's message .... free_rtn(D4DK)
	spl: block/allow interrupts .... spl(D3D)
	srv: service queued messages .... srv(D2DK)
start:	start access to a device .... start(D2D)
	start: start access to a device .... start(D2D)
uio(D4DK) iovec: data	storage structure for I/O using .... iovec(D4DK)
	strategy: perform block I/O .... strategy(D2DK)
qreply: send a message on a	stream in the reverse direction .... qreply(D3DK)
limit value/ module_info:	STREAMS driver identification and .... module_info(D4DK)
structure streamtab:	STREAMS entity declaration .... streamtab(D4DK)
msgb:	STREAMS message block structure .... msgb(D4DK)
datab:	STREAMS message data structure .... datab(D4DK)
information structure qband:	STREAMS queue flow control .... qband(D4DK)
procedures structure qinit:	STREAMS queue processing .... qinit(D4DK)
queue:	STREAMS queue structure .... queue(D4DK)
declaration structure	streamtab: STREAMS entity .... streamtab(D4DK)
log driver	strlog: submit messages to the .... strlog(D3DK)
queue or band of the queue	strqget: get information about a .... strqget(D3DK)
a queue or band of the queue	strqset: change information about .... strqset(D3DK)
buf: block I/O data transfer	structure .... buf(D4DK)

Permuted Index 13

Permuted Index

cred: access credential	structure .... cred(D4DK)
datab: STREAMS message data	structure .... datab(D4DK)
hdedata: hard disk error data	structure .... hdedata(D4D)
map: private memory map	structure .... map(D4DK)
identification and limit value	structure /STREAMS driver .... module_info(D4DK)
msgb: STREAMS message block	structure .... msgb(D4DK)
convert page frame number to page	structure page_numtopp: .... page_numtopp(D3DK)
queue flow control information	structure qband: STREAMS .... qband(D4DK)
queue processing procedures	structure qinit: STREAMS .... qinit(D4DK)
queue: STREAMS queue	structure .... queue(D4DK)
STREAMS entity declaration	structure streamtab: .... streamtab(D4DK)
uio: scatter/gather I/O request	structure .... uio(D4DK)
copy kernel data using uio(D4DK)	structure uiomove: .... uiomove(D3DK)
ureadc: add character to a uio	structure .... ureadc(D3DK)
remove a character from a uio	structure uwritec: .... uwritec(D3DK)
iovec: data storage	structure for I/O using uio(D4DK) .... iovec(D4DK)
driver's message/ free_rtn:	structure that specifies a .... free_rtn(D4DK)
page_pptonum: convert page	structure to page frame number .... page_pptonum(D3DK)
strlog:	submit messages to the log driver .... strlog(D3DK)
execution of an event sleep:	suspend process activity pending .... sleep(D3DK)
completion of block I/O biowait:	suspend processes pending .... biowait(D3DK)
wakeup: resume	suspended process execution .... wakeup(D3DK)
display a driver message on	system console print: .... print(D2DK)
an error message or panic the	system cmn_err: display .... cmn_err(D3DK)
SAMESTR:	test if next queue is same type .... SAMESTR(D3DK)
message datamsg:	test whether a message is a data .... datamsg(D3DK)
buffer	testb: check for an available .... testb(D3DK)
for a specified number of clock	ticks /delay process execution .... delay(D3DK)
convert microseconds to clock	ticks drv_usectohz: .... drv_usectohz(D3DK)
drv_hztousec: convert clock	ticks to microseconds .... drv_hztousec(D3DK)
a specified length of time	timeout: execute a function after .... timeout(D3DK)
untimeout: cancel previous	timeout(D3DK) function call .... untimeout(D3DK)
buf: block I/O data	transfer structure .... buf(D4DK)
adjmsg:	trim bytes from a message .... adjmsg(D3DK)
test if next queue is same	type SAMESTR: .... SAMESTR(D3DK)
structure	uio: scatter/gather I/O request .... uio(D4DK)
ureadc: add character to a	uio structure .... ureadc(D3DK)
remove a character from a	uio structure uwritec: .... uwritec(D3DK)
storage structure for I/O using	uio(D4DK) iovec: data .... iovec(D4DK)
uiomove: copy kernel data using	uio(D4DK) structure .... uiomove(D3DK)
up an I/O request into manageable	uiomove: copy kernel data using .... uiomove(D3DK)
from the head of a message	units dma_pageio: break .... dma_pageio(D3D)
timeout(D3DK) function call	unlinkb: remove a message block .... unlinkb(D3DK)
in bytes to size in pages (round	untimeout: cancel previous .... untimeout(D3DK)
structure	up) btopr: convert size .... btopr(D3DK)
useracc: verify whether	ureadc: add character to a uio .... ureadc(D3DK)
	user has access to memory .... useracc(D3DK)

copy data from a driver to a	user program copyout: .... copyout(D3DK)
copyin: copy data from a	user program to a driver buffer .... copyin(D3DK)
segmap: map device memory into	user space .... segmap(D2K)
access to memory	useracc: verify whether user has .... useracc(D3DK)
allocate a message block	using a shared buffer esballoc: .... esballoc(D3DK)
data storage structure for I/O	using uio(D4DK) iovec: .... iovec(D4DK)
uiomove: copy kernel data	using uio(D4DK) structure .... uiomove(D3DK)
a uio structure	uwritec: remove a character from .... uwritec(D3DK)
request physiock:	validate and issue raw I/O .... physiock(D3D)
driver identification and limit	value structure /STREAMS .... module_info(D4DK)
address getvec: get an interrupt	vector for a virtual feature card .... getvec(D3D)
memory useracc:	verify whether user has access to .... useracc(D3DK)
bp_mapin: allocate	virtual address space .... bp_mapin(D3DK)
bp_mapout: deallocate	virtual address space .... bp_mapout(D3DK)
address kvtophys: convert kernel	virtual address to physical .... kvtophys(D3D)
/get an interrupt vector for a	virtual feature card address .... getvec(D3D)
device mmap: check	virtual mapping for memory mapped .... mmap(D2K)
vtop: convert	virtual to physical address .... vtop(D3D)
address	vtop: convert virtual to physical .... vtop(D3D)
rmsetwant: set the map's	wait flag for a wakeup .... rmsetwant(D3DK)
rmwant:	wait for free memory .... rmwant(D3DK)
set the map's wait flag for a	wakeup rmsetwant: .... rmsetwant(D3DK)
buffer after block I/O and	wakeup processes /release .... biodone(D3DK)
execution	wakeup: resume suspended process .... wakeup(D3DK)
message datamsg: test	whether a message is a data .... datamsg(D3DK)
useracc: verify	whether user has access to memory .... useracc(D3DK)
queue for this module or driver	WR: get pointer to the write .... WR(D3DK)
write:	write data to a device .... write(D2DK)
driver WR: get pointer to the	write queue for this module or .... WR(D3DK)
	write: write data to a device .... write(D2DK)

Prentice Hall, the leading publisher of C and UNIX® System V reference books and documentation, is continuously expanding its channels of distribution in order to make book buying as easy as possible for professionals for whom access to timely information is crucial. Won't you help us to serve you more efficiently by completing this brief survey? Individuals completing this survey will be added to our C and UNIX® System bookbuyer list and will receive our new C and UNIX® System Catalog and other announcements on a regular basis.

Title Purchased: _____
Author: _____

I. **How did you purchase the book?**
   ___ by mail ___ by phone ___ by fax
   ___ in a bookstore ___ in a software store
   ___ through a corporate book distribution service
   ___ at a professional meeting or seminar

II. **Was this purchase charged to your business?**
    ___ Yes ___ No

III. **Are you involved in developing and/or instructing training courses?** ___ Yes ___ No
     If so, please provide the following information:

     Course Title: _____
     Number of Students Per Year: _____
     Books in Use: _____

IV. **Are you interested in packaging UNIX System V documentation with your product?**
    ___ Yes ___ No

V. **Would you like to receive information about our custom documentation program?**
   ___ Yes ___ No

VI. **Please list topics of importance to you and your colleagues on which you would like to see books published:** _____
    _____

VII. **Are you interested in submitting a manuscript to Prentice Hall for possible publication?** ___ Yes ___ No Area of Research _____

Name _____
Title _____
Name of Firm _____
Address _____

NO POSTAGE
NECESSARY
IF MAILED IN THE
UNITED STATES

BUSINESS REPLY MAIL

FIRST CLASS   PERMIT NO. 365, ENGLEWOOD CLIFFS, NJ

POSTAGE WILL BE PAID BY ADDRESSEE

PRENTICE HALL
Attn: PTR Marketing Manager
College Marketing Department
Route 9W
Englewood Cliffs, NJ 07632-9940